Praise for *All Is Calm*ish

"With warmth, wisdom, and a voice that feels like a trusted friend, Niro Feliciano reminds us that the holidays don't have to be perfect to be meaningful. *All Is Calmish* offers the grace and guidance we need to embrace the season with more ease and less stress."

—**Craig Melvin**, cohost of NBC's *TODAY* show

"Niro Feliciano is a voice I trust completely when it comes to my life and relationships. I'm so thankful this book is in the world so others can be impacted by what she has to say."

—**Rachel Cruze**, #1 *New York Times* bestselling author, podcast host, and financial expert

"Niro Feliciano gets it—our stress, our striving, our deep desire to make the holidays meaningful without losing ourselves in the process. *All Is Calmish* is the kind of book that takes your hand, reminds you to exhale, and gently leads you back to perspective. With wisdom, honesty, and heart, Feliciano walks with us toward a season that feels lighter, freer, and true to who we are."

—**Julie Lythcott-Haims**, *New York Times* bestselling author of *How to Raise an Adult*, *Real American*, and *Your Turn: How to Be an Adult*

"As a therapist who has worked with kids and families for three decades, I can say unequivocally that the holidays are one of the most stressful seasons of life for us all. Parents, kids, grandparents, aunts and uncles, humans—none of us are exempt. The time with the most pressure to be happy and connected often serves as a microscope for all that's not. But it doesn't have to be. Thanks to the wisdom of my dear friend Niro Feliciano, we can be honest about all that the holidays are—and are not. We can be present. We can participate in a true sense of wonder. We can reconnect to a place of hope. And we can find our own version of calmish. This book will help you discover how."

—**Sissy Goff**, LPC-MHSP, therapist, bestselling author of *The Worry-Free Parent*, and cohost of the *Raising Boys and Girls* podcast

"If you've ever tried to understand how to navigate life's chaos with clarity, then you need this book, because Niro Feliciano has put all of that wisdom in one place. *All Is Calmish* is the guide we all need to find peace in the midst of the holiday madness, no matter what life throws our way. This is the book you will want year-round, but especially for the holidays!"

—**Tamsen Fadal**, journalist, podcaster, and *New York Times* bestselling author of *How to Menopause*

"*All Is Calmish* is filled with equal parts wisdom and warmth. I quickly devoured this read about how to enjoy the special moments we spend so much time preparing for. Feliciano has a knack for weaving together personal insights, professional expertise, and compelling narratives. Although this book is perfect for the holidays, I know I'll be recommending it throughout the year!"

—**Saumya Dave**, psychiatrist and author of *The Guilt Pill*

"Anytime Niro Feliciano speaks, we listen. Whether it's parenting, family dynamics, or social interactions at home or at work, Feliciano's advice is always spot-on, practical, and actionable. Her book is full of real-life holiday scenarios and solutions. A practical survival guide and helpful read!"

—**Vicky Nguyen**, cohost of NBC News Now and *New York Times* bestselling author of *Boat Baby*

"Although the holidays are intended to be a time of meaningful connection and enjoyment, they can be full of stress and pressure. What if it could be different? What if you had a wise, steady, trusted guide to help you find your way to something more peaceful and hopeful? You are holding a road map, written by a gifted clinician and mother of four, who will feel like your new best friend. This should be a required read for every one of us before the holidays arrive each year."

—**David Thomas**, therapist, bestselling author of *Raising Emotionally Strong Boys*, and cohost of the *Raising Boys and Girls* podcast

"Some people just radiate calm—and Niro Feliciano is one of them! Now she's letting us in on her secret to letting peace and joy reinvigorate a busy home. Holiday stress has met its match, and I'm so thankful for this powerful guide written with the wisdom of an expert and the tender heart of a best friend."

—**Kari Kampakis**, bestselling author of *Love Her Well* and *Yours, Not Hers*, and host of the *Girl Mom Podcast*

"Niro Feliciano is the real deal—wise, compassionate, and no-nonsense when it comes to helping you let go of stress and overwhelm. *All Is Calmish* is like having a therapist and a best friend reminding you to set boundaries, drop the guilt, and actually enjoy the holiday season. If you're done feeling drained by the holidays, this book is a must-read for finding balance and peace and reclaiming your joy!"

—**Terri Cole**, psychotherapist, author, and podcast host

All is CALMish

HOW TO FEEL LESS FRANTIC AND MORE FESTIVE DURING THE HOLIDAYS

NIRO FELICIANO, LCSW

Broadleaf Books
Minneapolis

ALL IS CALMISH
How to Feel Less Frantic and More Festive During the Holidays

Copyright © 2025 Niro Feliciano. Published by Broadleaf Books. All rights reserved. Except for brief quotations in critical articles or reviews, no part of this book may be reproduced in any manner without prior written permission from the publisher. Email copyright@broadleafbooks.com or write to Permissions, Broadleaf Books, PO Box 1209, Minneapolis, MN 55440-1209.

30 29 28 27 26 25   1 2 3 4 5 6 7 8 9

Library of Congress Cataloging-in-Publication Data

Names: Feliciano, Niro author
Title: All is calmish : how to feel less frantic and more festive during the holidays / Niro Feliciano, LCSW.
Description: Minneapolis : Broadleaf Books, [2025]
Identifiers: LCCN 2025002796 (print) | LCCN 2025002797 (ebook) | ISBN 9781506498348 hardback | ISBN 9781506498355 ebook
Subjects: LCSH: Happiness | Contentment | Self-realization | Mind and body
Classification: LCC BF575.H27 F435 2025 (print) | LCC BF575.H27 (ebook) | DDC 158--dc23/eng/20250318
LC record available at https://lccn.loc.gov/2025002796
LC ebook record available at https://lccn.loc.gov/2025002797

Cover image and design by Sydney Prusso

Print ISBN: 978-1-5064-9834-8
eBook ISBN: 978-1-5064-9835-5

Printed in India.

To Raji and Satchi:
The greatest gift has always been having parents like you.

CONTENTS

A Note to You, My Dear Reader	1
1. I *Am* Freaking Merry!	7
2. A Silent ~~Night~~ Morning	15
3. The "I Get To" Shift	23
4. Snow Days	29
5. A Season of Thanksgiving	33
6. Great Expectations	41
7. What to Expect When You Are Expecting . . . a Holiday	49
8. Angels in Our Midst	55
9. Choosing Joy	61
10. Finding Strength in Uncertainty	67
11. Faith over Fear	73
12. Snapshot of the Sleigh Ride	77
13. Eight Great*ish* Nights	83
14. Contentment. For Life	89
15. Connected and Content	95
16. Holiday Drama 101	101
17. The Three Ds of Holiday Conflict	105
18. Is Less Really More?	111
19. The Empty Seat	117

20. A Perspective on Pain	123
21. The Holiday A-List (A Is for Anxiety)	127
22. A Reset for the Season	133
23. Unexpected Gifts	139
24. Disappointing Gifts	145
25. A Tale of Two Christmases	151
26. Presence over Presents	159
27. To Holiday Card, or Not	165
28. If You Believe	171
29. Wonder	175
30. Miracles in the Mess	181
31. New Year, Same Me	187
Ten Ideas to Keep the Holidays Simple and Memorable	193
Acknowledgments	197
Notes	199

A Note to You, My Dear Reader

IT'S THE HOLIDAYS, and I am well aware that you don't want to add one more thing to your endless to-do list. Who needs more to do this time of year?

But let me ask you this: how much of *last* year's list do you remember? What memories from last year's season come to you right now, at this very moment? What do you actually recall about last year's holiday?

If you are anything like me, you are hard-pressed to remember a single significant moment from the last winter holiday season. That would require some serious mental magic, especially with my perimenopausal mind. I normally need to search the 39,197 photos saved on my phone (not joking) to trigger a memory that casts a warm holiday glow—one that, if I'm lucky, might soothe my already frazzled nerves triggered by tacky Christmas mall decor in October. Come on, I know I'm not alone here.

As a therapist, I can say that few escape the holiday stress, even those who adore it—and trust me, I do. And in addition to the busyness—running from the winter choral concert to the office cocktail party when you just want to go home and get into your cozy pj's instead of the tight velvet dress that necessitates some serious Spanx (ugh!)—all the issues we have dealt with over the last year rise to the surface during this season. Loneliness, grief, financial stress, strained relationships, family drama, and of course year-round, old-school anxiety. Maybe you're lucky if you are feeling calm*ish*, because that's a lot of *ish*!

If you read my first book, *This Book Won't Make You Happy*, you know why issues like loneliness, anxiety, and depression have increased in intensity: culture. The relentless pressure to do more, to have more—and in December, to give more and to get more—swirls ever faster. During the holidays, those pressures, which are intense all year-round, push us up against the confines of this seasonal snow globe. Can we make the holiday memorable? Can we craft our way to festive? Can we make it all happen? And what if the well-planned plan doesn't go as planned?

What many of you don't know is that this book was originally set to come out a year ago. That holiday season was anything but calm for us. I wrote many of these chapters with a heavy heart because one of my children was suffering with debilitating anxiety and needed me more than ever. Every day proved unpredictable. Would she get out of bed? Could I get her to school? Would she stay in school so I could work? Fear sometimes got the best of me: would she ever get past this and have a normal life again? All of me, my time, and my energy were focused on supporting her, and writing this book became nearly impossible. The combination of this stress and the holidays at times felt insurmountable.

I had very little left to give to anyone that year, and joy was hard to find.

Like me that year, many of you have very real life stressors layered on top of holiday pressures. One thing I have seen in nearly two decades of practice as a psychotherapist is this: for many reasons during the holidays, our mental, physical, and emotional health takes a hit. Unless we know what to do that can help make a difference in our wellness, it will be hard to enjoy this season.

This is why I wrote this book—a book that you will likely read only one month out of the whole year. But that's enough for me. And I hope it's enough for you. Let me tell you why.

What if this holiday could be different? What if this year we didn't get sucked into the vortex of overdoing and decorating, overspending and stressing? What if we gifted ourselves a meaningful holiday full of memorable moments of joy—ones that we could easily call to mind, year after year? What if we could create a carol of calm that melodically resounds in our minds this season? And what if we held on to a perspective on what really matters every day for the next month—and try to let go of what doesn't?

I believe we can do this together. As a mom, as a therapist, and as someone who has carefully orchestrated every detail of seasons past, I'm here to talk you through it all. At the end of the holidays, we are tired of being tired. Let's do it differently this year, learning from psychological research, science, and the timeless wisdom of spiritual traditions.

The two consistent comments about my first book from readers around the world were that after reading it, they felt like they spent several hours with a good friend. Many wrote that they could actually hear my voice. I never imagined that book would find its way into office waiting rooms, schools, hospital psych wards, cafés, vacation spots, and homes of all shapes and sizes. But the one thing I prayed for was that people would find it when they needed it the most. The stories I received in letters, emails, and messages about how people found this book were nothing short of miraculous. Readers wrote to tell me that they felt less alone and more understood. They began to see a way to do life a little differently, even if it meant being a little kinder to themselves. I also learned from their notes that finding calm and perspective in our most stressful hours will always be priceless.

So, at a time of year when most of us feel stressed, many of us feel alone, and some of us even feel desperate, I'm here to literally talk to you every day. Start when you need it—maybe around Thanksgiving or at the beginning of December—and go at your own pace. If you are looking to hold on to perspective for a whole month, I've crafted thirty-one chapters for that purpose. Consider doing it with friends to keep each other calm. I want you to feel the wonder this season has the power to release into our lives. We have the ability to create a fulfilling, meaningful holiday experience if our focus is directed toward the right places. *Hint:* the real magic is often found in the ordinary which becomes extraordinary when seen through a clear lens and felt with a calm heart.

In this book, there is something for everyone. If you are looking for inspiring holiday stories to lift your spirits, they're here. Need tips to manage family issues or holiday anxiety—I got you. If you are struggling with grief in this season, my dear friend shares her story so you can know you aren't alone. Take what resonates and leave the rest. If you miss a day, take your time to catch up, or skip to what you need, or just open it up to a random page and perhaps it will speak to you. No need to fake feeling festive; come as you are.

Each chapter includes a section titled "Baby, Stay Calm Inside" with specific ideas to try. This is *not* a checklist, and you will find that I ask more questions than I give answers. Although you will hear my voice, hearing *your* voice is what's more important. Uncovering your deepest desires is central to creating the holiday you want.

Lastly, you will find a section titled "Soul-Full Season" in some of the chapters. For those of you for whom this season is sacred, or for those who are looking to embrace spirituality or experience greater faith, I have included prompts for added reflection. Faith has always been central to how I understand the world, and you will hear that at times in this book. As a therapist, however, I also write from a research-informed perspective. So, no matter what your beliefs are—faith or not—you are welcome here. I hope there will be parts that strongly resonate with each of you.

My hope is that what you begin now will transcend this season and turn into a life of simple practices and rituals that enable you to carry the peace, the presence, and the perspective you find within these pages into all seasons.

Ready? Well then, let's get this holiday party started. (Also, know that if you are truly my people, you will definitely come late and dressed in those cozy pj's.)

1

I *Am* Freaking Merry!

IT'S THE MOST wonderful time of the year. Yet if I could caption the expression on the faces of the people I pass as we rush around Main Street of my Hallmark-esque, holiday-lit small town—well, it would be the title of this chapter.

Maybe you can relate? For years I had these holiday goals that I promised myself I would fulfill the following year: Start planning earlier. Start wrapping earlier. Don't buy so much. Don't eat so much. Do less. Enjoy more. Don't get sucked into drama. Focus on what matters!

And every year I found myself getting swept up by the current of holiday excess, being pulled down by the undertow of unhealthy patterns of Christmases past, fighting to come up for air, and gasping for a silent night at the end of the season.

Until one day I said, "No more."

I wish I could tell you which Christmas it was, but when you operate at that level of exhaustion, they tend to blend together. What I do remember is this: whatever year it was, my husband Ed and I were up until 4 a.m. on December 24th. That evening had already consisted of a candlelight service, followed by the family dinner we had hosted with my parents, sisters, and a few close friends. Now, it was time to get ready for the big day . . . at 11 p.m.

We had four kids under the age of ten, and Christmas was, hands down, the highlight of the entire year. We loved our kids' excitement, and we did not want to disappoint them. As we tried to get mostly everything on their lists; chose different wrapping papers for each kid, according to their interest; and, of course, motivated the elf to do something festive and funny—we certainly made efforts to make it magical.

The interesting thing is that neither of us had grown up with lavish holiday celebrations. Both of us are the children of immigrants, and we grew up in very different situations but with surprising similarities. Ed was poor, having been born to Puerto Rican parents who moved to the mainland in their late teens. Gifts were not the focus, and he does not recall holidays being stressful or unpleasant.

My parents came here from Sri Lanka in the 1970s as physicians. Planning to move back to Sri Lanka, they saved most of what they earned during our childhood with the intention of creating a better life back home for them and their families. I recall receiving one special gift and a few small ones, but there was no making an extravagant list with the hopes of receiving every wished-for item. Holidays felt happy and joyous. I remember enjoying family time; simply having all of us home together felt special. With two doctor parents, we knew that sometimes holidays meant that one spent the day on call in the hospital, so having everyone at home together was by far the best gift.

Somewhere along the way, however, between our own childhoods and our children's, Ed and I apparently forgot the wisdom and joy of a simpler holiday. Early on, our holiday celebrations morphed into something quite unrecognizable.

To pull off a festive, detailed, gift-filled Christmas, you really have to begin before we did. Starting to wrap presents at nearly midnight on Christmas Eve is true torture. Every year, I got to that moment and discovered that the pile of gifts to be wrapped outnumbered what I had envisioned. My husband and I would have the same conversation:

Me: "This kid has way more than this one. Ugh!"

Ed: "They all have too much. This is unnecessary. Why did you buy so much?"

Me: "I forgot I had bought some of this. It just gets so crazy. I have to keep better track next year."

Ed: "We say this every year! (By *we*, he means me.)"

Midnight on Christmas Day is not the most productive of times. I don't even know what we were doing *that* late. Likely finishing up the twelve different kinds of cookies we'd helped the kids leave out for Santa before they went to bed. (I'd also peeled the carrots for Rudolph and his friends—seriously, why do I peel carrots for reindeer? I don't know, but I do it *every year*.) And probably perfectly placing the gifts that we had just wrapped around the tree—because three- and five-year-olds really care about the aesthetics of symmetry and pattern, right?

As we crawled into bed, hating Christmas and ourselves, I swear I only closed my eyes for ten minutes before I felt a small creature bouncing on my belly.

"Mama! It's morning!" (It wasn't.) "Saaantaaa!" squealed the high-pitched tiny voice.

"Jesus," I mumbled. I wish I had meant that in the Christmas sense. (I didn't.)

Later, as my kids got older, they learned my one Christmas rule: we don't go downstairs before 7 a.m. Now, it's harder to wake up the teenagers than me. But back then, neither pitch-black darkness outside nor catatonic parents could stop them.

That year I wanted to feel joy. I longed to feel merry. Instead, I could barely lift my head under the weight of exhaustion, dehydration, and sleep deprivation. I sat on the couch, my eyes barely open wide enough to see my beautiful, biracial babies in their fuzzy-footed pajamas, tearing open their gifts with excitement. It didn't take much in those years to bring them to delirious delight: a baby doll in its crib, a set of colored pencils nestled in a glittery case, a wondrous truck with flashing lights and a piercing siren (which is not wondrous seven minutes later). The sparkle of the fairy lights on the tree paled in comparison to their little faces each time they opened even the smallest of surprises. Before me, beyond the lids of my drooping eyes, was a scene of such childlike joy and wonder, multiplied times four.

Suddenly, I heard the deep, guttural vibrations of my dear husband's inimitable snore. I looked over at the couch next to me at the source of the auditory assault on the festivities. He'd always been a great sport about my night-before madness, so I couldn't blame him; I was barely awake myself.

This was not what I wanted for us or our kids. They were growing out of these types of magical mornings right before our eyes. Were we going to let this happen year after year? Get so busy preparing for the holiday that we'd be too tired to actually enjoy it? Were we going to sleep our way—literally—through these days?

Like many low points in my life, this "aha" moment prompted a decision. When I hit these moments, I usually ask myself, "What am I supposed to get from this? What's the message here?" I'm a big believer that if we miss the message, we will be taught the same lessons, over and over again, until we get it. Look for it when you hit your lows. Those messages serve as life's GPS directions. We need them to get to the next stop on our journey.

My message that day resounded loud and clear: you are missing it. The goodness, the sweetness, the beauty, and the joy of this season: you are missing it. All of it.

I decided flat out, there on that couch, that no longer would I miss it because I was too tired.

miss it because I was too busy.

miss it because I was preparing for too many next holiday events.

miss it because I was distracted by less important things.

I knew that I longed to be present—truly present—to take in the wonder surrounding me.

I see that eye roll. I hear your doubt. Is being present even possible for working parents with kids? Especially during the holidays? To be totally honest, for most of us, being fully present even 50 percent of the time feels impossible. But that doesn't mean we can't become more present more often. We can choose the moments that we know we want to hold on to and make sure we show up—awake—for them. It begins with identifying them and then preparing accordingly.

Is every holiday calm and manageable now? Am I constantly full of energy and joy? Definitely not. There are moments of calm, joy, and excitement, and also some of stress and exhaustion. That is holiday normal. But I don't wrap presents at midnight any longer because I have chosen to be present the next morning. I have made sleep a goal in December. I also say no to things I don't really care about far more readily than I used to. That took

> **There are moments of calm, joy, and excitement, and also some of stress and exhaustion. That is holiday normal.**

a little practice. Is the holiday perfect now? Far from it. But I'd choose presence over perfection any day.

> **Is the holiday perfect now? Far from it. But I'd choose presence over perfection any day.**

The stories and practices you will read in these pages have helped me to gain perspective on how to experience the holiday in a meaningful way. Creating a fulfilling holiday meant taking a hard look at my expectations, shifting my mindset, choosing my focus, and letting go of the events and people that drain my joy. In working through this book, I might just ask you to do the same.

But let's start with what's most important to *you*.

Baby, Stay Calm Inside:
- What are three moments that you would like to be fully present for and engaged in this holiday?
- What do you want to experience in these moments?
- What might have to change to make that happen?

2

A Silent ~~Night~~ Morning

DURING THE HOLIDAYS, late nights often turn into *running late* mornings. You know those too early alarm clock mornings, those "five more minutes" at 6:30 a.m. that turn into "How is it seven fifteen already?" It is nearly impossible to cultivate an atmosphere of calm if catching up becomes the goal from that first tap of the snooze button. If you are anything like me, unless you have a good reason to get up early, such as the bed being on fire, sleep will always win.

In a season of relentless noise and constant flurry, a morning ritual that allows for some much-needed quiet time can be *just* enough to motivate me to drag my feet out from under the warmth of the covers and into my fluffy leopard slippers. As alluring as the first sip of hot coffee, a few moments of silence to gather my thoughts and reflect have become something I look forward to, especially during the busiest time of year.

The key here is to create a ritual that is meaningful to you based on what you need, what you enjoy, and what will help you feel calm before you hit the ground running. If you are not a morning person, perhaps your ritual is better suited to the evenings, before bed, or a short break in the middle of your day. You choose the time that is best for you to create a moment of peace. There is research, however, that suggests there are mental health benefits of a morning ritual, especially one that involves time for silence and reflection.

My morning ritual always involves light. During an interview with the inimitable Oprah Winfrey, novelist and physician Abraham Verghese revealed that anytime a friend asks him to pray for someone, he lights a candle.

"So do I!" Oprah said, delighted to learn of this shared ritual. From Tibetan monks' meditations, to Catholic cathedrals' memorials, to a household Hanukkah menorah, candles are central in sacred traditions in every culture and religion. Lighting a candle changes the energy of a space. The mesmerizing flicker of gentle flames focuses the mind and relaxes the spirit.

> **Lighting a candle changes the energy of a space. The mesmerizing flicker of gentle flames focuses the mind and relaxes the spirit.**

Get ready, because I'm about to drop some med school–dropout knowledge: fire is all about energy change. Fire is the chemical reaction in which potential chemical energy is converted to kinetic energy, otherwise known as the energy of motion. I love this principle that fire represents literally releasing potential into motion. What a powerful symbol of what could await us each day!

In fact, I began writing each chapter of this book by first lighting a candle with the hope of releasing wisdom into these pages. However you decide to begin your ritual, I would suggest starting with soothing light. It may be the light of your favorite candle with a scent carrying you back to cherished memories of holidays past, or the soft glow of your Christmas tree, or perhaps the sparkle of your menorah. Holiday light sets a tone of calm that ushers us into the meticulous workings of the day with a little touch of magic.

If you live in warmer climates, I encourage you to begin your day with a walk, soaking in the soft illumination of morning light. Sunlight early in the day regulates our circadian rhythms and stimulates the synthesis of vitamin D, which has been proven to improve both mood and sleep.

Mornings for me always include coffee. But I strongly suggest drinking a whole glass of water as you are making your coffee or tea. We wake up dehydrated, and it's not uncommon to be more dehydrated during busy seasons. As you may well know, dehydration is a common culprit of fatigue, sleeplessness, and unhealthy food cravings, which can result in weight gain. Because self-care often goes by the wayside during this time of year, a little hydration can go a long way.

After my glass of water, I find a cozy spot with my coffee, light my candle, and sit by my fake tree with a few books. (I was the only one in my family on Team Fake Tree, but I won.) Any book will do. Even fifteen or twenty minutes of this type of self-care can positively impact the rest of your day and give you something to look forward to in the mornings. Fifteen minutes of reading is doable for most of us if we replace the twenty-five minutes of scrolling we do at some point in the day.

Your morning routine may include reading a great book for pleasure, one that transports you to a faraway place. My books include a gratitude journal and a devotional. This is my time to sit in silence and become aware of my own thoughts. I talk to God, give thanks, release a few worries, and, for a few minutes, simply breathe deeply. My very simple gratitude journal features three or four things in bullet point form that I appreciate about the previous day or this particular holiday so far.

We will never feel satisfied when we get what we want if we can't appreciate what we already have.

You will read more on gratitude and why it is essential to a fulfilling holiday in the following chapter. Whatever you choose to do, carve out a few minutes to reflect on what is already good in your life. We will never feel satisfied when we get what we want if we can't appreciate what we already have. (Sidenote: If this is a new concept for you, I wrote a whole book on it. It's pretty good. Check it out.)

You may want to include uplifting or peaceful music in your ritual. I love holiday music—but only starting on Thanksgiving! (This is a battle I fight with my oldest daughter and resident Buddy the Elf, Natalia, who breaks out the holiday tunes right after Halloween. Please! Can we even have a Thanksgiving around here?) Yet from the classic choruses of the *Messiah*, to the preternatural sounds of George Winston's *December* album, to toe-tapping Harry Connick Jr., and, of course, my playlist would not be complete without old-school Mariah Carey, holiday music can set whatever mood you need for the day.

One more suggestion: include a few minutes of stillness at the start or end of your ritual. Our culture does not value stillness as we continually strive to do more, be more, and have more. If sitting still and doing nothing is a new practice, you'll likely find it incredibly hard at first. Stilling our constant racing thoughts and sitting in silence will feel unnatural. Yet both ancient wisdom and psychological research advocate for this practice.

The health benefits alone compel us to consider silence as important as diet and exercise. Did you know that those of us who are exposed to constant noise increase our risk of high blood pressure, heart attacks, and even strokes? Physician Luciano Bernardi found that as little as two minutes of silence inserted between relaxing musical pieces proved to be more beneficial to stabilizing the cardiovascular and respiratory systems than the actual relaxing music. In addition, research out of Duke University School of Medicine revealed that silence encourages the growth of cells in the hippocampus, the area of the brain associated with learning and memory. If you, like me, sometimes can't even remember what you did yesterday, it's time for some silence in your ritual.

When we make time for silence, those thoughts we easily avoid begin to come to the surface. You may not want to take on those thoughts during the holidays. But during times of silence, the peace and presence of mind needed to cope with those issues may also appear. You may even find long-awaited solutions suddenly within reach, emerging out of the silence.

Although sitting in silence is difficult, stay with it. Start with a few minutes and build from there. My time of morning silence is usually less than ten minutes long. Your mind will wander, but you can gently bring it back to whatever you "hear" in the silence. This short practice will train your brain to be more present during the times most important to you later on.

I hope you can see that silence is powerful; it calms and strengthens both the mind and the body. Morning silence often gently ushers in moments of clarity when we need it the most.

> ***Soul-Full Season:*** If you are a person of faith, you may know that God usually doesn't speak loudly in the noise of life. The psalmist encourages us to "be still" so we can align our souls to the whispers of wisdom (Psalm 46:10 ESV). Spend five minutes in stillness today and note how you feel afterward. Include five minutes of stillness at the start of your ritual and take a few notes on what

comes to mind each day. It's amazing what you can hear when you make the time to truly listen.

Baby, Stay Calm Inside:
- What daily ritual will you look forward to this holiday?
- What would a good start to your mornings look like? (Here are a few ideas: sitting in silence, reading, listening to music, meditating, praying, journaling, relaxation breathing, going for a nature walk, and writing a note to someone you care about.)
- Start by deciding how much time you would like to spend on your daily ritual and then allocate time to the practices that will help you to start your day well. (Note that your ritual does not have to be in the mornings or even daily, but rather a few times a week or weekly. Everything counts!)
- Commit to a starting date and begin!

3

The "I Get To" Shift

HOLIDAYS WITH KIDS require supernatural powers, especially for moms and single parents. Most of us already run at max capacity all year long. I don't know about you, but I haven't heard many people asking, "What am I going to do with all this extra time?" Most of us don't have it. For that reason, our to-do lists in December resemble those endless CVS receipts that are long enough to use as scarves. And who really wants those?

A few years ago, the stress of the season felt heavier than usual. I found myself reluctant to do the things that once brought me joy or at least were supposed to bring me joy. They now had become items on my holiday to-do list that I anxiously longed to check off. I'm not sure if it was that I actually had more to do that year or simply that these holiday things had become a production. I blame social media. *I need to make a hot chocolate bar. We should go see the town tree lighting. Can't miss that holiday gift pop-up shop!*

Thanks to social media, most of us are now very aware of all the holiday things that we should be doing. We see them constantly every time we touch our phones. Then there's the added stress of *Do I post this? How does it look? How do I look? I can't post this! Why do I even care about posting?*

Just trying to make it to a very expensive, energy-draining finish line of some magical holiday is not a good way to spend our time. Yet, so many of us move through December much like this.

As a cognitive therapist, I have seen, over the course of two decades, exactly how powerful thoughts can be. If we can become aware of our thoughts, we can receive valuable insight into our feelings, giving us a better understanding of our behaviors. Yet, often our thoughts are so automatic—so fast—that we don't even realize we are having them, let alone hear what they actually sound like. When we start feeling differently about ourselves, our relationships, or our lives, it's important that we ask this question: what am I *thinking*?

Here's what my internal monologue sounded like that holiday, when I began to realize that I didn't have the same joy or motivation that I once felt: *I have to see eleven patients tomorrow. I have to stuff two hundred Christmas cards tonight. I have to find teacher gifts, and I have to make the cookies. Oh, and now I have to clean up this huge mess in the kitchen.*

It's not hard to see the pattern there, is it? Each sentence sounds like a chore. If it sounds like a chore, it will feel like one, too.

As I took a breath in the middle of my monologue, something stirred within me. Just a subtle whisper, but it was powerful enough to make me stop for a moment.

Oh no, not I have *to. I get to.*

What if I just tweaked my internal holiday chatter?

I get *to help eleven people who trust me enough to share the most difficult details of their lives. I* get *to send Christmas cards to people who have touched my life in some way. I* get *to clean up my kitchen after my four kids who were all with me for dinner—kids who got off the bus after school and are healthy enough to make this huge effing mess.* (Just keeping it real for you. This is what went through my mind.)

In psychology, we call that a *reframe*. Reframing my tedious tirade changed my perspective. Completely. What *felt* negative felt that way simply because I had failed to recognize my privilege and even my blessings. And let me call myself out: these are 100 percent problems of privilege—First World problems, as I call them, especially when my kids are complaining. But this is exactly why we need a perspective shift: we need to realize we are privileged to even *have* some of these problems.

The impact of this shift was almost instantaneous when I realized that someone, maybe even in my world, would do anything to have my stressors. This is not to minimize anyone's pain or stress. Stress is stress, and we have to feel our feelings, not repress them. We need to empathize with ourselves and practice self-compassion first. But sometimes a perspective shift is just enough to move

Sometimes a perspective shift is just enough to move through the stress and even flip the script.

through the stress and even flip the script to see the overwhelming good hidden in the midst of it.

Listen: this perspective shift won't work for every situation that is distressing. No one is asking you to say, "I *get* to spend the holidays grieving my loved one," or "I *get* to be unemployed this year," or "I *get* to hand off my kids to my ex on Thanksgiving and spend it alone." No.

But maybe there is a different *get to* waiting to be discovered, alongside the sadness of those incredibly difficult seasons. Maybe we get to experience the unexpected kindness of good people who care about us going through grief. Maybe we get to spend some precious moments with our kids because we may be forced to spend more time with them, like when they are home instead of school because of anxiety. Maybe we get to spend this holiday with a friend and find a different kind of joy in that.

Lastly, let's talk about "should" statements. If you read my last book, you know how I feel about "shoulding" all over yourself. Don't do it, and especially not during the holidays. "Should" statements create pressure and expectation that often add stress and leave you feeling guilty. A simple rephrasing of this desire can make a difference.

Replace the phrases *I should* or *I need to* with these phrases: *I would like to*; *If I have time, I will*; *It would be nice to*. Instead of saying, "I should watch holiday movies with the kids," change it to "I would like to watch holiday movies with the kids." Do you feel the difference? This quick phrase exchange releases the pressure but honors the desire.

Small cognitive changes can bring surprisingly big perspective shifts that will help you move through the holidays—and hopefully the rest of the year—with a little more ease.

Baby, Stay Calm Inside:
- Name three "I have to" statements that could become "I get to" statements this season.
- How are you "shoulding" on yourself? Can you rephrase any of your obligations so they truly reflect what you desire?

4

Snow Days

A SNOW DAY. Before Christmas. In the month of December. For the working parent—or any parent, really—it might as well be a natural disaster.

I looked around my house as the reality of four kids at home set in. Boxes of Christmas decorations yet to be hung, laundry to be folded, groceries to be bought, meals to be planned, gifts to buy, cards to address, and emails to be answered: each thought triggered a new wave of anxiety. And let's not forget that now there were kids to be fed every hour—and I mean on the hour.

I took a deep breath and tried to tackle the next right thing, only to be interrupted once again.

"Can we go sledding?" begged my six-year-old, Carolina.

"Absolutely! In a little while. How about a Christmas movie?"

"Yay! Will you watch it with us?"

"Yes, in just a bit." But I knew they would forget, and I might have a chance at getting *something* done, which I did. But it didn't take long until they were back.

"Can we pleeease go sledding?" whined my eight-year-old, Sofia.

"Yep, in just a little while. How about writing a letter to Santa?"

I knew my big kids would help the little ones, and I just might be able to clean out the fridge and answer a few emails, which is part of my usual Monday routine. Lucky for me, one thing led to another. They played, they drew, they fought, and they played a little more as the day flew by.

At one point, I glanced at the clock, and it was 4:30 p.m. The sun was setting, gently casting blue-gray shadows on the pristine, newly fallen snow.

"Mama, can we go sledding *now*?"

And now, at dusk, it was now or never.

"Yes, of course! Get dressed and I will watch you from the window."

"But Mama, we want to go sledding *with you*." Both little girls looked at me with their pleading eyes—big brown eyes that I gave them.

I knew I had to go.

I paused. I looked around at boxes still unpacked, dishes to be done, dinner not yet cooked, and the snow day mess abounding. But this time, instead of my mental checklist on repeat, I heard something different. What I heard was that still, small voice that I'm learning to trust, the one that gently whispered, "How much longer will they want to do this *with you*?"

Because I had older kids, I knew it's just that quick. The little whiles turn into tomorrows, and the tomorrows into weeks, and the weeks into years, and it all happens in a blink. Everyone tells you this, but one day you begin to feel it, and it's a feeling that stays for a long while. Before you know it, they are taller than you, stronger than you, busier than you, and have more important things to do than spend time with you.

> **It's just that quick. The little whiles turn into tomorrows, and the tomorrows into weeks, and the weeks into years, and it all happens in a blink.**

In that moment, I realized this was not an *I have to*; it was an *I get to*. Because there are thousands of women who pray they will get to go sledding on a snow day with their kids—and never do. Because even in December, moms lose babies, single parents have to work late, chemo treatments continue, cars don't work, kids split holidays, and the ocean of grief only gets deeper.

So, I dropped everything and put on my boots, gloves, and hat, and we went sledding. Because isn't that what this season is about? Dropping everything to go and witness the extraordinary in the ordinary?

We made our way through the darkening shadows in the snow, climbing our backyard hill. I breathed in the cold, crisp air and watched as the girls threw themselves down to create snow angels. Their laughter echoed loudly through the leafless branches, lit by the rising moon, and, right then,

I thought, *This must be the most peaceful place on earth.* For a moment I just stood there, taking in the wonder and glory of my everyday miracle.

My very own silent night.

I took a mental snapshot, to be tucked away in the corner of my holiday memories, and I hoped my daughters would remember this day, too. Because I can't recall the gifts or the wrapping or the carefully placed ornaments of my own childhood. But I will always remember the love and the laughter and the mess—the joyous, colorful, comforting post-Christmas mess that never bothered me one bit.

So, once in a while, drop everything and go. Say yes every chance you get, while you still have the chance.

Because long ago at Christmas, the most extraordinary thing happened in the ordinary, and it still does today.

One thing I know: it will be your best yes yet.

Baby, Stay Calm Inside:
- What is one thing that may be inconvenient but that you want to say yes to this holiday?
- What do you have to let go of to make this happen? Why is letting that go worth it to you?
- If you need some ideas for simple, memorable moments, check out the list at the back of the book and see if anything appeals to you

5

A Season of Thanksgiving

IN MY HOUSE I do everything in my power (which is diminishing now that I have teens) to hold on to Thanksgiving. Aside from a day of eating carbs upon carbs with a side of carbs until everyone falls asleep on a couch, Thanksgiving is a day to reflect on what is good. There is no pressure to give anything, which greatly reduces the possibility of ending the holiday in disappointment. It's a day to gather and spend time with friends and loved ones and just appreciate that you made it through another year and have another holiday to celebrate together.

If you ask my kids, they will tell you what I love most is going around our table hearing what each person is grateful for—even if it's the same thing year after year. Perhaps you do this at your table too? As we get older and evolve, our lists evolve, too. As we age or if we have watched loved ones fight hard against illness over the past year, we no longer take health for granted. When we have aging parents, we stop time and take in the image of their presence at our table. As we approach the empty nest, we might experience a wave of sudden gratitude along with nostalgia as we look around at our big kids who still live with us, now with an awareness that it's truly only for a moment.

And, of course, simple things that make us happy in the moment always make the list. For our family, this includes our annual boozy Thanksgiving Yamallow. (BTW, Yamallow never makes us happy on any other day of the year. Never. Who came up with this yearly vegetable/cocktail/dessert?)

I know that not everyone experiences Thanksgiving like this. For many, it is the first day of the season of stress—a reminder of a rapidly ticking clock. We begin to count the weekends we have left to get everything done before Hanukkah or Christmas. Family drama comes to the forefront as we navigate tricky interactions that we managed to avoid all year. The funcle and the drunkle make their appearance at the holiday table. (Many of us have both the fun uncle and the drunk one, although sometimes they are one and the same.) We are forced to share spaces with difficult people who trigger our nervous systems before they have even said a word.

It's not joyful people who are grateful; it's grateful people who are joyful.

So, in light of this reality, I ask you to sit with this thought for a moment: it's not joyful people who are grateful; it's grateful people who are joyful.

I don't remember where I heard this, but I can tell you that I have seen it in practice and in life thousands of times over. Gratitude is the direct pathway to joy, not the other way around. Social scientist and author

Brené Brown says she recalls not one interview out of twelve years of research and eleven thousand pieces of data in which a person who described themselves as joyful did not actively practice gratitude.

The numbers are compelling. If you are facing a tough holiday ahead, remember that gratitude is also the direct pathway to something even more powerful: resilience, which is our ability to move through and move forward with greater strength and wisdom.

It makes sense, then, that if we want a joyful holiday, or at least one in which we can protect our peace, gratitude must be at the center. If you talk to grateful people, you will find that gratitude is a *practice* and not merely a *feeling*. For those who have made it a regular practice, gratitude becomes a *mindset*. The remarkable thing is that when this practice becomes a way of life, we see significant physiological changes that enable us to not only feel happier but live longer and healthier, too.

In Spanish, Thanksgiving translates to "Día de Acción de Gracias," which literally means "Day of Grateful Actions." Gratitude requires action to fully reap the benefits. What if we made this an entire *season* of grateful actions? How would the season change? Science tells us that our minds and bodies would certainly feel the difference.

There are a few ways to practice gratitude that will change the way you feel. The good news is that none of them take a lot of time, so you can still do them in this busy season. They will also direct your focus in these next weeks.

Why? Because you will begin to almost unknowingly scan your environment for good things. And when you look for them, you will find them. This practice will determine how you experience this holiday and how you remember it in the future as well. Is it worth spending five minutes of your day on gratitude? I think so!

Research out of UC Berkeley describes what your brain looks like when you are grateful. We know that different "gratitude actions" actually release different mood-elevating neurochemicals in the brain. Expressing thanks to someone or showing gratitude through a note, a gift, or a kind act bathes the brain in dopamine. Dopamine increases motivation and productivity and gives us a momentary high. Do this often enough, however, and it's not just momentary; it's a solid way to elevate your mood. Writing or journaling about what we are thankful for releases serotonin, which is a natural mood enhancer and stabilizer.

When we engage in these behaviors repeatedly, our brain structure changes to develop more neural pathways to support it. This is the beauty of neuroplasticity, which simply means our brain's constant adaptation to a changing environment. By making gratitude a regular practice—perhaps two minutes in your morning ritual—you can rewire your brain to release these neurochemicals. In other words, we can absolutely rewire our minds for happiness.

As I mentioned, people who engage in these practices also live physically healthier and longer lives. Research shows that cardiac patients who kept gratitude journals for eight weeks had lower levels of inflammation and reported to experience better sleep and less fatigue. Why is this? (If you are happy to just take my word for it and are not into "the science," just skip the next paragraph.)

Stress triggers a stress response within the body, which is treated like a threat. The body then responds as if it were an emergency. Remember fight or flight? Even though it's just the stress of holiday shopping, the body still prepares itself as if it needs to run away from a wild boar. Hormones such as cortisol, adrenaline, and norepinephrine are released. If stress is prolonged, high levels of these hormones over time can cause inflammation, which weakens body structures (such as heart vessels and arteries) and is associated with many illnesses such as autoimmune diseases, cardiovascular disease, asthma, depression, Parkinson's, GI disorders like IBS, and even some types of cancer. When cortisol is constantly high, systems in the body like the hypothalamic-pituitary-adrenal (HPA) axis can become dysregulated as they attempt to lower levels of stress hormones, causing important immune functions to be compromised in the process. Immune cells, such as natural killer (NK) cells, are our frontline defense against cancer, and they are suppressed during longer periods of stress. So, you can see why the body has a harder time fighting illness when you are stressed. Do you tend to get sick during the holidays or soon after? This may be one reason why.

Gratitude not only releases neurochemicals that elevate our mood, but it also enables us to find perspective and cope with stress. As a result, we see lower levels of stress hormones. Regulating stress hormones means optimizing immune function. This is why people who practice gratitude live longer and healthier.

This fun fact about gratitude is especially important to remember during the holidays when stress abounds. Seriously, don't hesitate to whip it out at a cocktail party. Point being, we can do something about stress in this season and some of these practices are quite simple.

Here are some ways to practice gratitude this holiday. You might want to pick one grateful action and practice it regularly. When we pair a new practice with something we do every day, like making morning coffee, it is called *habit stacking*. When we wire in something new with something already in our routine, it's more likely to stick.

Journaling: Take three minutes in the morning while you are making your coffee or tea to jot down three things you are thankful for. The key is to find things specific to the present. So, instead of saying "my home," "my health," or "my kids," ask yourself: *what about these things do I appreciate?* For example, you may say, "the cozy blanket on my couch," "the sweet holiday ornament my child made for me at school," or "the fact that I felt strong at the gym today." Keep your journal close by on your kitchen counter as a reminder.

Expressions: Send a text of thanks or appreciation for something someone has done. Or just let them know what their relationship means to you.

Conversations: Share three good things out loud with your friend, partner, or family around the dinner table. These can be wins, things that you are grateful for, or just simple, good things. If you do this with a friend, set a regular time to check in, even if it is only for five minutes a week.

Shared Gratitude Note: I love the practice of sharing a note on the Notes app on your phone with friends or family. I do this with my sister and daughter, and ours is called "Good Things Are Always Happening to Me." Each person periodically adds something they are grateful for, which keeps everyone accountable and inspires gratitude among the group. And it's fun to see good things happen in the lives of those you love.

Memories: Lastly, this Thanksgiving and at other events during this holiday season, take a mental snapshot of each person who is there with you. Think of something about that person that makes them unique and, if it's someone you are close to, what you love about them. Let your thoughts linger there for a while. If you feel bold, tell them. You never know where life may take any of you next year, so appreciate this moment right now. I promise, one day, you will be so glad you did.

Baby, Stay Calm Inside:
- Which gratitude practice is most doable for you this season?
- Where can you make time for it in your schedule? Morning, lunchtime, evening?
- With what other habit could you stack this practice?

6

Great Expectations

WE ALL HAVE them, don't we? Realistic or not, said or unsaid: when it comes to the holidays, we hold on to expectations tightly, year after year.

Mine sound like this:

> "I won't overspend this year."
>
> "I'll do it. It won't be too much work. I have time."
>
> "This is the year he really will find the perfect gift."
>
> "I'm not going to eat junk this holiday."
>
> "I'm sure they will try to get along—it's just one day!"
>
> "The kids are going to love this!"

Famous last words, right?

Expectations are not harmless. We hold them for ourselves, our loved ones, and our experiences. These very expectations have the power to determine if we will have a holiday that is enjoyable and peaceful or stressful and disappointing. For this reason, it's of utmost importance that we take a good look at our expectations as we begin the season. The good news is, if we can identify our expectations and modify the ones that were never realistic in the first place, we have the power to take back control of how we may feel this holiday.

In June 2002, my now husband Ed proposed to me just ten days before being deployed as a flight surgeon on an aircraft carrier to the Middle East. Do you remember 2002? Those were the days of no social media and no smartphones. (My twenty-six-year-old self loved that Nokia flip phone!) For six months, we had very limited contact because of both lack of technology and Navy security protocols, but we did send emails back and forth a few times a week.

As difficult as it was to be apart, life was simpler then. We lived our lives more in the present, without the constant draw of comparison culture at our fingertips. We waited with anticipation and much expectation for the day we would be together once again.

That day arrived a few days before Christmas, on December 19. Ed was stationed in Norfolk, Virginia, and I was living in New York City. I decided to drive down a few days before he returned to Norfolk and decorate his house for the holidays. That way he and his housemates, who were also deployed, would come home to some Christmas cheer.

For weeks I looked for symbolic ornaments to represent their travels afar. I found sparkly old-fashioned jets, hand-painted glass American flags, Uncle Sam snowmen, and glittery globes with world maps. They would adorn the Christmas tree that I was planning to buy when I arrived in Virginia. What a perfectly patriotic surprise they would walk into! I couldn't contain my excitement.

And, of course, it had to be a real tree. (I hadn't yet discovered the magic of a fake tree and a winter wonderland pine-scented candle . . . that came *after* the four kids.)

I really didn't know where to go look for a tree once I got to Virginia. The landscape was a far cry from every tree-farmed corner in New England, where I had grown up. So, I made the obvious choice and stopped at Home Depot, where I knew they would tie the tree to the top of my Jeep. Perfect!

In my excitement, however, I didn't stop to consider how five-foot me (on a good day) would get the tree *off* the car. By myself. Without scissors to cut the rope that tied the tree to the car.

Just picture me trying to pull a seven-foot, well-secured tree off the roof of my SUV. I can still recall branches flying everywhere and picking needles out of my blown-out hair, which was growing curlier by the minute in the humid Virginia evening air. This was the closest I have ever come to wrestling an alligator.

Finally, I managed to drop the thing onto the pavement. Then, like a caveman who has just killed a lion and is headed back to the cave, I started dragging it toward the house. With my Christmas plaid scarf and my hair now two feet wide in the eighty-degree weather, I must have looked like Mufasa on his way to a tree lighting.

"Do you need help with that?" a male voice called out from the darkness. It turned out to be one of Ed's friends who was taking a walk in the neighborhood and saw me. He helped me carry the tree inside and set it in a stand. I said a silent prayer of gratitude for the serendipitous rescue, thanked him profusely, and started to decorate.

A few hours later, I stood in front of the decorated tree, admiring my somewhat disfigured but delightful Christmas creation. It was late now, around midnight, so I headed upstairs to set out my outfit I had carefully planned for the next day. One thing I knew was that after six months of separation, I was going to look cute when that aircraft carrier arrived. After a seven-hour drive and a five-hour tree fiasco, I knew, too, that I would sleep well.

I didn't know that I would sleep *so* well that I didn't hear the crash in the middle of the night. In the early hours of daylight, I walked downstairs in Ed's house to see my tree leaning not quite on the ground but almost. Half of my meticulously chosen ornaments lay cracked and broken in pieces on the wooden floor beneath it.

I wanted to cry. But I knew tears would make my eyes puffy, and vanity always wins with me. So, I swept up the mess and salvaged what I could, rehanging many of the ornaments with the broken sides against the pine branches. Good enough! I ran upstairs and quickly got ready to leave.

If you have ever seen an aircraft carrier come into port, you know that it is an amazing sight. The ship looks majestic and regal, like a floating silver city. There are five thousand sailors on board, so you can imagine the massive crowd of families awaiting their arrival. I was one person among thousands. With Christmas six days away, this was an extra special delivery for all of us.

As I mentioned, it was warm. But I had planned my outfit with a Connecticut holiday in mind: black leather fitted flared jeans, a cardinal red sweater, and a black velvet duster-length jacket. We had an approximate time that the carrier would come in, but after we'd waited for an hour, there was no sight of it. However, what did appear were thick, ominous clouds that swirled directly above us.

One thought that never crossed my mind was the potential for rain. We didn't have smartphones that could check the weather, so unless you watched the news, knowing the forecast wasn't a thing. Of course, it didn't just rain; it torrential downpoured. Leather, velvet, and I were soaked. I looked like a wet cat. This definitely was not the holiday homecoming I had envisioned.

A nice man with a graying beard in a pickup truck nearby saw me shivering as the rain turned cold, and kindly invited me to jump in and wait in his dry cab. Normally, I wouldn't jump into the pickup of a stranger, as my anxiety brain would warn me that this could be an axe murderer. But my Jeep was parked quite far away, and I didn't want to die of hypothermia before I saw Ed. (As I said, anxiety brain.)

As we waited, we chatted about this gentleman's son, who was "finding himself" in the service, how it seemed to be giving him a sense of purpose. During Ed's time in the Navy, I gained incredible respect for these families who made big sacrifices to serve, many who would not be with their loved ones over the holidays. This loving father clearly missed his son and had such hopes for the man he would become. Mid-conversation, my phone started to ring. I saw Ed's name on the screen. I hadn't received a call from him in months, so I knew the carrier must be close enough to shore that he now had a signal.

"Go outside! I'm waving. At the top."

I quickly thanked my rescuer and jumped out of the truck. In the distance, I could see an enormous gray mass approaching the shore. The cheers of the dense crowd began to rise until they were deafening. On the very top of the carrier on the flight deck, I could see a tiny, lone figure in a flight suit. He was holding a cell phone to his ear and waving.

And suddenly none of it mattered. The mangled tree, the broken ornaments, my soaked outfit: I forgot them all in that instant. He was home safe.

The Navy has a beautiful tradition of letting the new fathers disembark the ship first. Each of those new fathers streamed past us, wearing their "New Dad" stickers with pride. (I imagine these days there would be some new moms, too). My eyes filled with tears to think of these parents who couldn't be present at the birth of their children, now holding them for the first time. It still makes me teary-eyed.

I continued to talk to Ed on the cell phone, so he could find me in the crowd. After what felt like an eternity, I saw him. I don't remember much after that other than a very long, strong hug. I thought he would never let me go. As soon as he released me, I was hoisted into the air by his 6'6" Australian American buddy, Damien—who to this day, twenty-three years later, will do the same thing every time he sees me.

Did that homecoming meet my expectations? Nope. This reunion was far from what I had envisioned. But over two decades later, I can laugh and say that, in many ways, it exceeded them.

There's more on expectations to come, but I'll end for now on the idea of acceptance. If we can accept the circumstances that we have no power to change, and hold on to what matters, we may find something different but still worthy and beautiful—and possibly a lot more

If we can let go of what should have been and embrace what is, we may find what needs to be.

memorable. If we can let go of what should have been and embrace what is, we may find what needs to be.

Soul-Full Season: When my expectations aren't met, I often go back to this thought: if we are constantly asking God to meet our expectations, how can God exceed them? Maybe we should start asking a different question.

Baby, Stay Calm Inside:
- Have you ever had a situation that didn't turn out as you had planned but ended up being better than you imagined? Revisit that moment.
- Do you have any tough situations you are facing in this season? What about these situations do you need to accept so that you can feel more peaceful this season?

7

What to Expect When You Are Expecting . . . a Holiday

WE NEED TO get back to expectations. I don't want to leave you hanging if you are now thinking of some of your expectations that are *never* met during the holidays. It's incredible how we still hold on to hope even when we know deep down that a particular expectation is unrealistic. Hope is a powerful, healing force. Yet it must be aligned with *realistic* possibilities.

Let's go back to some of the common holiday expectations that I listed in the last chapter:

> "I won't overspend this year."
> "I'll do it. It won't be too much work. I have time."
> "This is the year he really will find the perfect gift."
> "I'm not going to eat junk this holiday."
> "I'm sure those relatives will try to get along—it's just one day!"
> "The kids are going to love this!"

If I just took five seconds and thought about how every holiday ends, I would know right away: if the list above were a true or false test, the answers would be very clear. So, even though I don't say these expectations out loud, and even though I might not even be aware that I hold them, I know they exist by how I feel when they are *not* met. If I don't rethink them, then I am going to be left disappointed, stressed, and even angry when the holiday circles big Fs on all my subconscious statements.

If I don't modify these beliefs, here is the emotional result. I am going to feel

>stressed if I have to pay off a large debt in January.
>tired if I don't have time and energy for the things that are most meaningful.
>disappointed with my husband if I don't like his gift.
>frustrated at myself if I choose to indulge.
>mad at my relatives if they create tension at the table.
>angry at my kids if they fight and don't appreciate all my hard work.

Since when was Santa's sack so stuffed with difficult emotions?

The truth is, all these things very likely could happen during the holidays. Failed expectations are very normal when we have gifts to buy and receive, more responsibilities than usual, family to see, and kids together for a longer period of unstructured time. Like it or not, we have to make room for all of it, but we will feel better when we do it with compassion both for ourselves and those around us.

We can rethink our expectations, so we don't set ourselves up for disappointment. It starts with recognizing that our fixed expectations often don't get met. Then we can modify our thoughts about these beliefs and give ourselves and others a little grace.

> **We can rethink our expectations, so we don't set ourselves up for disappointment.**

My revamped list might sound like this:

> "I will do my best to set a budget and try to stick with it. There may be some areas that I go over, but I can pay it off over the next few months. That may mean I have to make some sacrifices."

> "I normally say yes to too much and then have no energy left for the things that matter. I am going to work on saying no and prioritizing the things that are important."

> "My husband loves me regardless of the gift he finds for me. He shows his love for me in many other ways. The gift may or may not be a reflection of that truth."

"I am going to try to make healthy choices, but it is normal to enjoy and indulge during the holidays, and I will make a plan to get back on track after."

"My family may not get along during the holidays, and I can't change them. I will think of ways to maintain my own peace during these moments."

"I am going to try to give my kids a fun holiday. They may not appreciate all my efforts, and there will likely be a fight or two. That is normal for kids, and I'm not the only parent who feels this frustration."

You may notice these new beliefs sound like mini conversations with ourselves. We need to have them. In doing so, we align our expectations with reality and then are a little more prepared to face it. We may still feel some disappointment, but we will not be left completely surprised by the outcome because we have made room for it.

As you speak these statements to yourself, you will find a little more understanding for your own human nature and that of others, too. This does not mean we don't do the work to set boundaries when needed and communicate expectations clearly (more on that in a bit). But we all fall short—sometimes especially when we are stressed. Changing expectations is one way to bring a little more calm to your holiday.

Baby, Stay Calm Inside:
- What expectations or beliefs do you have for yourself, your family, or other people in your life that often don't get met? (For example, *Family time is peaceful, and everyone enjoys it.*)
- How can you rewrite these expectations so that they are more realistic and don't leave you as disappointed?
- What can you do (that depends only on you) to bring yourself more joy during the holidays?

8

Angels in Our Midst

IF YOU ASK people in Connecticut what happened on December 14, 2011, most of us will know. That day remains deeply etched in our forever memories. Most of us will recall exactly where we were standing, frozen, the moment we heard the news that twenty angelic first graders and six dedicated educators at Sandy Hook Elementary School were killed.

Sandy Hook is a fifteen-minute drive from where I lived at the time. That holiday season was simply like no other one I have ever experienced. My heart still aches thinking about the excitement of the children in school just days before the holidays. About the parents who had wrapped their gifts early, which would now remain unopened. Although this quintessential New England town twinkled and tinseled, the weight of grief hung heavy in the air.

In the midst of the fear, rage, and sorrow that enveloped the community, the residents came together to help the families and each other in every way possible. People volunteered any way they could, donating whatever they had to help someone affected by this searing loss. From school children across the country making snowflakes to send in solidarity to restaurants catering meals night after night for families from Sandy Hook, everyone wanted to help.

Therapists are called to action in these times. We don't have any words or formulas to alleviate this depth of suffering, but we are trained to walk alongside people to help them navigate trauma and hopefully, eventually, find a measure of peace.

Like most clinicians in the area, I spent hours upon hours talking to families, schools, and churches in the aftermath of the tragedy. I listened and counseled and explained trauma and offered tools to manage the anxiety that rippled through the neighboring towns. My work was far more than a *desire* to help; I *needed* to help. As a mother of three young kids under five years old, I needed a way to step out of my own fear and sadness by helping another through theirs. This was something that I could do at a time when so many of us longed to do something. When we find that we have something that we can offer others, it begins to clear a path forward out of helplessness into hopefulness.

> **When we find that we have something that we can offer others, it begins to clear a path forward out of helplessness into hopefulness.**

I learned during that time that we are *designed* to help others. Christopher L. Kukk, author of *The Compassionate Achiever*, defines compassion as empathy plus action. Compassion is the ability to feel what another feels and then do something about it. When we step into action instead of simply empathizing, the image of our brain changes. MRI images of the brain during empathy look like those of someone in pain. However, when we see images of the brain during compassion, they look like those of someone in love. Compassion releases mood-elevating neurochemicals, such as oxytocin—the hormone we see in the brains of mothers and babies as they bond and also in the brains of humans who feel connected to another.

One evening a few days before that Christmas of 2011, I received an unexpected call from my friend Jen.

"How are you, Niro?" she asked. I think that was the first time in weeks someone had asked *me* that question. It took me by surprise so much that it brought tears to my eyes. I had seen that happen when I asked women this question in therapy sessions, and suddenly I understood why.

"I'm okay. Tired, sad, but I can't complain. I can't even imagine . . ." My words trailed off. Even though my situation felt hard, I knew it was nothing compared to the grief of those around me, especially those who lost their precious children. I felt guilty for feeling bad even for a second.

But I often tell my patients that there really is no hierarchy of pain; we cannot compare our pain to that of others. You can have empathy for another's suffering and still acknowledge your own challenges. In fact, pretending your own pain isn't so bad will eventually create more suffering in your own life. It's good to say that life often feels hard, even when you know someone going through something harder. The first step in working through difficult emotions and getting to the place where we can appreciate what is also good, is naming our pain.

So, I did admit it to my friend: I was tired, I told her. Exhausted, really. A practice full of patients with holiday stress, in addition to caring for my young family, in addition to helping out with a local tragedy with national reverberations: it was more than a lot. Not to mention trying to get ready for a holiday that no one really felt like celebrating—least of all me.

After I'd talked for a while, Jen said, "My mom and I were thinking that you must not have much time these days, and we want to bring you and your family dinner tonight. You have been doing so much for everyone else. We want to help you."

My eyes filled with tears, again. *No one helps the helpers*, I thought. To be honest, I didn't even know how to receive her offer.

"But why? I'm okay, really."

Jen paused. "We want to do it," she said gently. "To thank you for what you are doing."

I knew Jen didn't have much time either, and it was now five days until Christmas. She had four kids herself, thus outnumbering me by one. (Although a month later, I found out I had caught up with her; I didn't know at the time, but I was in the first few weeks of my fourth pregnancy.)

That evening Jen and her sweet mom arrived at our house, arms overflowing with the most delectable BBQ—which was even more delicious because I hadn't had to cook it. For what felt like the first time in weeks, someone gave me a moment to breathe. To sit with my family. To *not* help.

I don't know what a real angel looks like, but the only one I've seen up close smelled like ribs.

I'm not even sure if Jen and her mom remember that night. Knowing them, I imagine such a caring act is not unusual. But that one thoughtful act has stayed with me for over a decade. I think about it every holiday, and I'm still genuinely moved, still grateful for the kindness I didn't even know I needed. Now, as a result, every holiday I look around to see who else needs a moment to breathe like I did.

One thing is true: You don't have to be healed to help, and, more often than not, helping makes way for healing.

You don't have to be healed to help, and, more often than not, helping makes way for healing.

Soul-Full Season: Do thoughts of someone randomly cross your mind? Often the Spirit will bring someone to mind for a reason. A simple text to check in and say "I'm thinking of you" can go a long way. Reach out and find out.

Baby, Stay Calm Inside:
- Have you ever received an act of kindness? If so, call to mind the details. If not, ask yourself, What would I appreciate someone doing for me right now?
- Is there someone you know this holiday who needs that support or a word of encouragement? You never know the kind of impact you could make.

9

Choosing Joy

I KNOW. ALL around you, the world is telling you to sing for joy. "Joy to the World" and "Happy Joyous Hanukkah" and all that. Yet joy is one of the last emotions you may feel right now in this season of busyness. There is nothing like nights of little sleep and days scheduled to the minute that suck the living joy right out of you.

The irony is that while many of us spend the holidays trying to create joy for others, it is often the hardest emotion to find for ourselves. One year, joy could not be found around our house. Literally.

For the last ten years, if you drove by our house at Christmastime, you would have seen three-and-a-half-foot tall letters that spell out J-O-Y hung on the front. My husband made the *J* and the *Y* by hand out of sturdy pine and painted them a vibrant cardinal red. The *O* is a softly lit wreath with white lights, which glow on wintery afternoons, welcoming my kids home off the bus. On our street, we are known for this outward *JOY* on our house, which you can see from the main road through the bare branches in the distance.

Yet one year, the letters would not stay affixed to the side of our house, no matter what we tried. Wind, rain, snow: they'd take out a letter in one fell swoop. Especially that darn *J*. Many days, I would drive home from my holiday errands to see a big *OY* on the side of my house. I'd joke with my Jewish friends, "Looks like we celebrate Christmas *and* Hannukah now!" We put that *J* back up so many times, only to have it fall off again, that by December 20, we simply accepted the following fact:

This was going to be the year of *OY*.

And boy, was it.

That year I felt less energetic and motivated than past years. Between travel for my kids' sports teams, middle-school friend issues, and family drama of the new and improved variety, I couldn't catch a breath.

Our regular life challenges don't stop just because it's the holidays, do they? These weighty situations clearly affect our ability to "put on" the holiday as usual.

Normally, I decorate three trees in our home. Now I know this is excessive. But, my kids love this season and how festive our house feels to them and their friends, so I try to do it every year because it brings them joy. That year, however, I managed to get one tree decorated, one up with only lights, and one up with working lights that only reached halfway down the tree. That last one was in my front window, and it stayed up well into February. In November, people would see it and ask if I was in the middle of putting up the tree; after the holidays, they would ask if I was taking down the tree.

To both questions, my answer was the same. "Sure . . ." I'd say and leave it at that.

Other years we would also bake and decorate several different kinds of cookies. When I say this year was half-baked, believe me: I even made cookie dough that never touched an oven. It's probably still in the back of my freezer somewhere. And when my sister texted me a photo of a cheese spreader that someone had left at her house after her holiday party, asking if it was mine, I had a good laugh. I can't even make this up. I looked down at the photograph, and there was my little red-handled knife—painted with the white letters *JOY* looking back at me. Joy literally didn't want to return to my house!

If you know me, you know that I always pay attention to the signs and messages around me. So, the timing of the events that I just described to you was not lost on me.

I knew it was no coincidence that I was scheduled on December 20 to speak on the *TODAY Show* about . . . wait for it . . . choosing joy.

One thing that I have experienced over and over again is this: if I am being called to give a message, I will be made to *live* that message. It's like God says to me, "I will make sure you practice what you preach!" This little life lesson enables me to live an authentic life, and although it has often caused me *great* frustration, I would have it no other way. No surprise: this proved to be the year *I* needed to choose joy.

So, here is the good news. Joy is a *choice*. In this life with all its challenges, if you want to experience joy consistently, you

Joy is the happiness that does not depend on what happens.

will have to choose it again and again. Here's the thing to remember: I said on the show that "Joy is the happiness that does not depend on what happens."

When we choose to do specific things that turn our lens to joy, we can elicit feelings of joy in our minds, hearts, and even bodies. The *feelings* of joy follow the *actions* of joy. We even see this neurologically with the release of dopamine, serotonin, oxytocin, and endorphins, depending on the action you take. Joyful people do not naturally feel happy all the time; they have simply made the decision to look for joy and choose it no matter what happens.

I want to share with you a practice that helped me feel joy the year it just wouldn't stay at my house. A colleague of mine introduced me to a five-minute meditation created by therapist Donald Altman that helped me to turn my lens to joy. It's a clever little acronym called GLAD:

G: something you are **grateful** for.

L: something you **learned** about yourself or someone else.

A: something you have **accomplished**.

D: something that brought you **delight**.

You might think of this as leveling up your gratitude practice. I began to write down short, bullet-pointed answers for each letter, answers that helped me to see not only what was good in my life but also what I accomplished. Many of us feel like we don't do enough each day, but we do *far* more than we realize every day in this season!

This GLAD practice also helped me to see the value in many interactions that I may have overlooked but in reality were quite meaningful. A short conversation when I bump into a long-lost friend in the grocery store, or my teenage daughter sitting on my closet floor, telling me about her day while I fold laundry: these are the sacred moments that connect us to one another. They are not expected, but they happen as we are doing life as planned, in between the plan and perhaps even more significant than the plan.

The D for *delight* took me by surprise. Delight is different than gratitude. For example, I am so grateful for my work; but my job is hard and stressful at times, and it does not delight me on a daily basis.

What delights you? This was the question that I began to ask myself, and it motivated me to begin to *create* moments of delight—just for me. And I want you to do that for you! Coffee with a friend, a nap under my comforting electric blanket, a cup of peppermint tea and reading a chapter of a good book on the couch: joy can be that simple.

When I think about what brought me the most joy during that year of *OY*, it was matching holiday pajama shirts for each of our family members, with sayings ranging from "Most likely to return all the gifts" to "Most likely to be late to Christmas." And seeing each person's face as they read their shirt? Priceless!

Of course, unexpected moments of delight can be exhilarating. But we can also create *intentional* moments in this season for our own joy. As the great Maya Angelou once said, "We need joy like we need air." We certainly do.

Soul-Full Season: Some of my greatest moments of unexpected joy came during my moments of stillness when I brought my stress, overwhelming feelings, and frustration to God. We need to be honest with ourselves about how we feel. We also can be honest with God about not feeling joyful. We can't just skip over the hard feelings. We often need to release our negative emotions and express them before we can feel joy. God promises to walk us through these tough seasons and give us peace. It starts with an honest conversation. Although that season of my life proved more stressful than others, there were moments of unexplainable peace that paved the way to joy.

Baby, Stay Calm Inside:
- Try the GLAD meditation above. Spend about three minutes on it. Connect it to a habit you do each day, perhaps when you wake up or before you sleep.
- What brings you joy? (Please think about this!) Can you include this in your week so that you look back on this holiday and remember joy?

10

Finding Strength in Uncertainty

I KNOW SOME of you are facing serious unknowns. These unknowns might leave you tearful, fearful, and weary. The holidays are the last thing on your mind right now, and some of you would ignore them altogether if you could. But instead they hang over your head, adding to the weight of your already heavy circumstance.

I have been in that place at this very time of year. I'm not trying to one-up you. And I'm not going to suggest that I understand what you are going through. When people assume they know "exactly what you're going through," I can relate to the great Anne Lamott, who so eloquently expressed her response to people who offer well-intentioned but clueless cliches: "I want to Taser them." I'm simply saying I know what it feels like when the holidays seem almost trivial.

When what's most important in your life hangs in the balance, holidays become an afterthought. And at these times, the support of loved ones matters more than we realize.

Holiday parties take a lot of work, but I do love to host a good one. I love to have my dearest friends and family in my home, to share my favorite holiday cocktails and mocktails—something sparkly with a touch of pomegranate—and to listen to familiar tunes that evoke memories of Christmases past. Hosting a holiday party always fills me with joy and gratitude.

But one such party nearly ten years ago stands out so clearly because of what came next. That night I remember looking around my home full of friends. People were laughing loudly, dancing, and celebrating life. Everyone looked so radiant with the glow of candles illuminating their faces. My heart felt very full and content. I felt so grateful for each person in my kitchen that night.

And I had no idea how much I'd need some of those people the very next day.

Then six-year-old Samuel had been begging us to go to the ice rink to try out his brand-new ice skates, an early Christmas gift from his grandparents. So, the next morning Ed and Samuel set off for the rink. Meanwhile, I helped our three little girls don their soft red velvet and satin dresses and get ready to meet Mrs. Claus for tea.

It was a magical morning, and later, on the way home, I received a call from my brother-in-law in Florida. He had spoken to Ed on the phone just a few minutes before.

"Are you home?" he asked me.

"Soon," I replied. "Why?"

"It's Ed," he said. "Something is off. He couldn't remember what he did yesterday."

How could Ed not remember yesterday? We'd had a party at our house! I began to feel warm all over, a telltale sign that my anxiety was about to make a grand appearance. But even my overactive, anxious mind could not have imagined what would come next.

I arrived home a few minutes before Ed walked into the house. A reddish-purple watercolor-edged halo circled his left eye. Just above it, a goose egg–sized lump seemed to grow larger the more I stared at it. "What *happened*?" I asked.

"I don't really know," Ed said, looking both amused and perplexed. "Apparently I fell on the ice."

Fifty questions later, answered between Ed and Samuel, I learned that someone had skated into Ed and that he had fallen on the ice and hit his head. There was a good amount of blood on the ice, which was scary for my second-grader son, and Ed was unconscious for a few moments. When the EMTs arrived, they checked him out and advised that he shouldn't drive after blacking out.

Years earlier, Ed's college roommate had said to me, "If you want to see Ed do something, tell him he can't do it." Sure enough, my darling husband—who had no memory of the fall—assured the EMTs that as an orthopedic surgeon, he could properly assess the situation himself. He signed the paperwork, against medical advice, that released him to drive home. Thank God we only live five minutes from the rink.

Doctors make the absolute worst patients, as you might know, and for the life of me, I could not convince this man to go to the ER. By this time, my anxiety had burned a hole through the roof of my house, as every possible worst-case scenario flashed through my mind. I finally convinced him to call a colleague, who said, "Ed, you know that losing consciousness is a red flag. You should go."

Hours later, the ER doctor's eyes were wide as he wheeled in a monitor to show us the images of Ed's brain. Ed had a small yet impressive brain bleed, for which he won a night in the ICU for observation. We would know by the morning if the bleed had grown, which may then necessitate brain surgery. If it stayed the same, he could possibly return home to rest.

Sometimes in life, time stands still. You wonder, Is this really my life? Or am I watching someone else's unfold in front of me? Is someone going to walk in the room and shout "Just kidding!" Less than twenty-four hours ago, we'd been celebrating, feeling a little tipsy and carefree. Now here we were, faced with an uncertainty that I never could have predicted.

I'll tell the rest of the story in the next chapter. It has a happy ending. But not all our stories do. When we're in the middle of our lives, we don't know how it is going to turn out. The unknowns are heavy.

That night in the ER, I did what I always do when I find myself in a situation beyond my control. I asked people to pray.

I started texting a few close friends to let them know that Ed had taken Samuel skating, had a bad fall, and now was in the ICU with a brain bleed.

True to form, our good friend Steve texted back immediately, "This is why I don't do shit with my kids." For the first time in hours, I laughed out loud. So did Ed when I read it to him. That text cut right through the fear and tension that permeated our tiny corner of the ER. We both needed that. Many people texted us kind, loving, and encouraging messages, many telling us they were praying.

We need people to walk with us through these times, in both humor and in faith. During therapy sessions, I have often reminded patients that it's okay to not have a strong, resolute kind of faith all the time. It's in those times we need to borrow the strength or the faith of others. When others loan us these gifts, it will cover us until we can find them again for ourselves.

Sometimes just knowing that people are with you and for you is enough to give you hope.

Baby, Stay Calm Inside:
- Are you walking through a tough situation? Is there anyone in your life who you can share this with who can help carry the weight of it with you, so you can feel less alone?
- Think about those friends or family in your circles who you know care and want to help. You'd likely want them to tell you if they were having a hard time. What would it take for you to reach out to one or several of them?

11

Faith over Fear

HERE'S THE BRIGHT side of anxiety: when the worst happens, you are already prepared.

Late that night in the ICU, eleven days before Christmas, I sat beside Ed's bed and finally accepted that I was not going to sleep at all. Ed was now hooked up to several monitors, and somehow he had settled into sleep. That man can sleep anywhere: I recall him snoring loudly when I was in active labor with our oldest, dilated to 7 cm, and now he was sleeping soundly in the ICU. I cannot. I sat in a chair watching him in the dim light of that hospital room, listening to the symphony of rhythmical beeps that filled the eerie silence.

But I was prepared. I had packed a small overnight bag for myself before we'd left home, and I'd thrown in a small devotional book. So, wide awake, I opened my devotional to the page for that particular day. The title of the reading was "Faith over Fear." *Hmm*, I thought. The author wrote that faith must be chosen, over and over again, in the face of fear. It wasn't a one-and-done choice.

I had always wondered what would happen to my faith in a situation like this one, in which the future dangles dangerously over a precipice. Would I choose God no matter what happened tomorrow or to our family? I wanted to believe I would, but I wasn't sure. Mind you, I give talks about faith and spirituality. I preach on occasion. People look at my faith as unshakable. But was it? I started to feel hot and fearful as those worst-case scenarios flooded my mind again, one after another.

Right then, I felt God speak to me. If this is a new concept to you, let me clarify what happens, at least for me: I don't hear God as an audible voice, but rather as a clear thought—one that sounds like my own, but somehow stands out from other thoughts and resonates with my spirit. It feels like I am receiving an important message.

What I heard that night was this: *What will* you *choose, Niro? Fear or faith? It's your choice.*

Over the next few minutes, as I sat with that message, I felt peace quietly slip into the room around me. When I thought back on my life, I realized that God had always been there for me, and I knew God would continue to show up for me no matter what life brought. No matter what happened, I couldn't imagine doing life without God. That was not an alternative I wanted to ever experience. I would choose faith.

I wish I could tell you that I stayed peaceful for the rest of the night. I didn't. All night my thoughts vacillated, tossing and turning along with my body upright in that pleather chair, alternating between fear and faith. Yet I knew that if I wanted faith, I had to choose it—just as my devotional reading had said—over and over again.

And so, I began repeating this mantra every time I felt fearful: "I'm choosing faith. I trust you, God." Again and again, I said it. Finally, in the early morning hours, I fell asleep.

In the morning, the doctors ran another scan of Ed's brain, and we learned that the bleed had not grown. A surge of relief flooded through my veins. I knew we would still have to watch and wait. I knew that in the days that followed, I would have to repeatedly make the choice to hold on to faith. In an instant, I felt in a new way how fragile life truly is. What was most important to me became as clear as the daylight that streamed into that hospital room in the early hours of the morning.

That holiday, a decade ago, we didn't buy all the presents we'd planned. We baked no cookies, and Christmas cards became New Year's cards. Yet an exhausted mom and dad couldn't have been happier. Perspective is the most precious of gifts.

Baby, Stay Calm Inside:
- Are you feeling fearful about anything right now? Is there an area of your life where you need to choose faith?

- Who can help you make this choice?
- Perhaps you need a mantra to help you get through this time. What could you repeat to yourself when fear sets in? Write it on a sticky note and put it where you will see it every morning, during the day, and in the evenings.

12

Snapshot of the Sleigh Ride

HAVE YOU EVER found yourself doing something you didn't want to do simply because other people were doing it? We must be extra careful about that in this season, because during the holidays, social media is extra curated and can often have an extra negative impact on our moods. Almost subconsciously, we hold up the reality of our messy, tinsel-tangled, not-so-extraordinary lives to the picture-perfect, carefully selected snapshots of others. The result is a mood-altering, perspective-changing experience that often leaves us feeling less than, not enough, and discontented.

Social media is a powerful driver of FOMO (fear of missing out). Just since I wrote my last book, researchers have developed a psychological scale to measure the level of anxiety that FOMO causes. FOMO can result in very real physical and emotional symptoms. In my work with patients, I am often amazed at how FOMO affects adults as much as teens alike.

In my house, all you have to say is "sleigh ride" for the memory of a holiday FOMO fail to resurface . . .

Just hear those sleigh bells jingling, ring ting tingling too . . . Oh, did I, as I scrolled through scenic images of friends on horse-drawn sleigh rides in Vermont on social media a few years ago. We had planned a weekend up north with the kids. While we are not great skiers (any activity that necessitates heated clothing to compensate for ice-cold temps while hurling yourself off high places is not my idea of fun), gliding through the glistening powdery landscape of Vermont in a horse-drawn sleigh seemed like ultimate holiday magic! Plus, we could get some good family photos for our Christmas card to preserve the memory of what was sure to be an enchanting day.

So, we bought the tickets. We'd get a horse-drawn sleigh ride with bells jingling and a stop halfway through to make s'mores over a bonfire in the woods. What could be better than that?

The day of the sleigh ride dawned cold and bright. When we arrived at the departure point, the woman at the counter said sternly and unapologetically, "It's far too cold for the horses, and there is too much ice on the path. So, we will be using a tractor to pull the sleigh."

A tractor?? What happened to my sleigh bells and my horses? The melodious soundtrack to our icy expedition would be the deafening whirr of a 1970s engine? Not exactly the holiday weekend—or photo—I had hoped for.

But we climbed aboard. At the very least, I had planned well for kids in the cold: I'd brought cozy blankets, warm wool scarves, and knit hats with fluffy pom-poms on top.

"Smile!" I said, snapping a quick photo before the tractor jolted forward with a loud lurch.

And we were off! After just a few seconds in motion, we discovered that the temperature caused the snot now dripping out of our noses to crystallize. Snotcicles. Awesome. Why did I think this would be a good idea?

Yet as I looked beyond the rustic wooden rails of the carriage, my heart slowly began to settle. It was golden hour, about an hour before sunset, and even with the unfortunate turn of events, the sun still cast a warm, coral glow on the frosted trails, which sparkled ahead of us for miles. In the distance, scattered patches of snow on the mountains glittered like the star ornaments my kids brought home from preschool art class. The beauty was breathtaking . . .

Literally. I tried to pause, breathe deeply, and take it all in—which was difficult with my snotcicle-filled nostrils and all. I turned to the kids to point out the magnificence of the moment . . . only to see all four of them—and Ed—with scarves pulled up over their noses and hats pulled down to meet them, completely covering their eyes.

I am not making this up.

The promise of s'mores kept my kids' hopes alive until the halfway point on this journey. I searched the path ahead, looking through the barren trees for the crackling bonfire somewhere in the woods. We desperately needed to defrost at this point.

By the time we arrived at the bonfire, eager to warm up near the heat of the flames, a strong wind had picked up. So much black smoke was billowing in our direction that we couldn't get anywhere near the fire.

Oh, and two of my kids have asthma. How was the ride back, you ask? *O'er the fields we go, coughing all the way.*

I tell you all this to say, you never truly know the whole story until someone tells you the whole story. From that photograph I took at the beginning of the ride—the smiling faces of my family, snuggling together under a blanket, with that whimsical, wintery landscape as the backdrop, the tractor carefully cropped out—you would never know that this was a complete and total holiday fail. You would never know that they complained all the way home about how cold and hungry they were.

Then again, it's also true that this is now one of my favorite holiday memories. Ed and I still laugh about it. But that just goes to show that what is *truly* memorable is not usually found in perfection.

> **Many people are going home to intense challenges, hidden behind closed doors—challenges that you would never know about from their social media profiles.**

As a therapist who knows the stories of many who appear to lead glamorous, easy lives, I can honestly say that no one is exempt from challenges. Many people are going home to intense challenges, hidden behind closed doors—challenges that you would never know about from their social media profiles. Perhaps if you did, you would be less willing to trade places with them, even for that one magical moment you may be seeing.

No, that day of the tractor-pulled sleigh ride was not a *real* challenge, but neither did that photo tell the whole story. So, please remember this truth when comparison or FOMO threaten to get the best of you in this season. Those snapshot moments are merely that: snapshots.

We all experience moments that are beautiful yet fleeting. Hold on to them. Tuck them into your back pocket. Take them out once in a while when you need to remember what you already have of true value. Maybe these moments don't involve an opulent holiday or a lavishly decorated home. Maybe we can find these moments in things like a sleigh ride gone wrong—which ultimately reminds us of everything that is right.

Baby, Stay Calm Inside:
- Do you find yourself comparing your experience of the holidays to other people's experiences? Do you feel dissatisfied with your life when you look at the lives of others through this lens?
- Consider taking a break from social media for forty-eight hours to a week. In addition to resetting your dopamine to healthy levels, the break from comparison will absolutely make a difference in how you feel.
- On your break, find things that feel fulfilling each day, and write these down. Look back at them at the end of your break. What feels different now?

13

Eight Great*ish* Nights

"THERE ARE VERY few holidays that last eight days!" exclaims psychologist Dr. Lisa Fraidin, my dearest friend and practice partner.

Lisa has some thoughts about the Jewish holiday, and she was willing to share them with me. "It's a tricky balance between trying to keep the kids happy and not going over the top while teaching them our values," she tells me. Can't I relate to that struggle! Over the nearly twenty years I have known Lisa, she and her family have graciously shared their cultural celebrations with us. We have had many interesting and beautiful conversations about our faiths and the similarities and differences between them. I didn't know enough about Hanukkah until we sat down to talk, but what I learned was so interesting. She has always told me that Hanukkah is not a central focus of the Jewish faith. Yet even so, this holiday brings with it both significance and challenges this time of year.

Unlike Christmas, for which most people have some days off work, Hanukkah happens alongside our normal busy lives. "Imagine working all day, seeing patients, driving to the kids' sports after school, coming home late . . . and squeezing in some sort of amazing celebration at the end of the night," Lisa tells me. "Oh, and then repeat that eight times. It's kind of like Groundhog Day!"

Perspective! Listening to Lisa, I have never been so grateful for just *one* overwhelming day of gifts! Eight is a lot for anyone to manage, and I can see why it can be daunting as the season approaches. Lisa explained that Hanukkah is not as significant to the Jewish faith as holy days such as Rosh Hashanah and Passover. Yet, kids often compare it to Christmas and hold similar expectations of gifts as their peers because it happens at the same time of year.

Comparison doesn't help. Lisa recalls the holiday when a friend texted her that she "has to get this toy, because all the kids have to have it." With the pressure of trying to come up with eight different gifts for each night of Hanukkah, Lisa was more than grateful for the suggestion. Of course, so was everyone else. This toy was sold out at every store within a fifteen-mile radius. Lisa finally found one, having driven an hour round trip. As she returned home, weary but filled with anticipation, she convinced herself the effort would be worth it, imagining her eight-year-old daughter's face lighting up with joy.

The night arrived for the big reveal. Lisa watched eagerly as her daughter unwrapped the long-awaited gift of the evening . . . only for her to burst into tears.

"I don't want this!" she cried, dissolving into a full-on meltdown.

In the moment, Lisa asked the question so many of us do: *Why am I doing this?*

"You know what we used to get?" Lisa asked me. "Underwear! That sleeve of colored knee-high nylons!" (And if you know what she's talking about, you are definitely in perimenopause.) But with her psychology background, Lisa understood her daughter and had compassion for how she felt. She didn't ask for this gift; it was the result of cultural pressure. She also knew how hard it can be for a kid to wait all year and then all day with high hopes, only to be disappointed.

For that reason, Lisa advises that we have to give ourselves grace. Eight nights of keeping everyone happy and celebratory is not easy. She has accepted that some nights will be great, some will be great*ish*, and some will be not so great. And that's okay. At the end of it, even though Lisa agrees that it isn't perfect, her kids still want the eight-night tradition in the way that she does it. They appreciate that it's what sets it apart from the Christmas holiday and what makes Hanukkah unique. It is incredibly freeing when you embrace the idea that "good enough" is both good and enough.

When I think of Hanukkah, I think of the traditional nine-branched menorahs, or hanukkiahs, illuminating winter windows with candlelight glow. Many people, especially those of us who celebrate Christmas, don't know that these candles represent a miracle that signifies the strength of the Jewish faith, the triumph of good over evil, and the faithfulness of God to bring deliverance against the odds.

As history recounts, the Jews were being persecuted and forced to abandon their religious beliefs and mandated to worship Greek pagan gods. Judah Maccabee and his family, a small group of fundamentalist Jews, led a long, arduous battle against the powerful Greek empire to defend their religious beliefs. They eventually won their independence. While restoring their desecrated temple and rededicating it to God, the Maccabees found a jar of oil. Although that oil was only enough to keep the menorah's candles burning for one night, the flames continued to burn for eight. This allowed the Maccabees time to find more oil and inspired hope among the Jewish people once again. Hanukkah literally signifies light in the darkness.

Much like we do with any commercialized holiday, we often lose this significance in the bustle of preparation and expectation. The strength of family and faith, a story of resilience and light: this often feels far from the way we celebrate.

Lisa recalls one of the most meaningful nights of Hanukkah, steeped in both family and tradition. Every year, her husband, Dov, prepares the traditional Jewish latkes, and the aroma of sizzling potatoes fills the air as the family gathers. Yet this night isn't just about the latkes: it is the warmth of family, the continuity of tradition, and the shared moments that make the night feel like the true essence of Hanukkah.

When we can see the reflection of our values and customs in our holidays, they become far more meaningful and memorable. That requires intention. Another friend of mine, psychologist Dr. Stacy Ullman, celebrates each day with such intention. Stacy covertly sets intentions and expectations by creating a theme for every night of Hanukkah. Cozy Night means books and pj's for everyone. For Charity Night, the kids research a new charity each year that is meaningful to them, and then Stacy and her husband make a donation in their name. There is an Experience Night, which is the gift of a fun family experience, such as a Broadway show, a thrift shop, or a local food tour. I personally loved their Sibling Night, when each sibling thinks of a special gift for the other.

Stacy is a creative and thoughtful gift giver and enjoys the process. Themes are based on her kids' individual interests, like sports and art and even coffee. How about an at-home barista machine for their college freshman? Stacy says her kids certainly put in requests, but they don't necessarily want to receive everything on their list. Instead, they anticipate with excitement the originality of the themes and the thoughtful surprises, all of which bring together their family and strengthen the bonds between them. (I've asked her to adopt me this coming Hanukkah.)

> **When we can see the reflection of our values and customs in our holidays, they become far more meaningful and memorable.**

Creativity and gifting aren't everyone's strengths, nor do they need to be. But when celebrating a holiday, it's essential to reconnect with what makes it meaningful to you. Ensure at least some of your focus remains on that, while letting go of the things that bring you no real joy or fulfillment.

Whatever your faith tradition, and whatever your celebration looks like, it seems that setting expectations and giving yourself grace need to be a part of the process. Because celebrating anything, while real life still happens, is a lot. And eight nights? I think great*ish* is great enough!

Baby, Stay Calm Inside:
- What do you love about your celebration that you want to hold on to or add, to make it more meaningful?
- Is there anything that does not serve you or your family any longer that seems to cause more stress than it is worth? How could you do it differently? Or can you let go of it altogether?

14

Contentment. For Life

I WILL NEVER forget a woman I met during one holiday season who exuded peace. In fact, she exuded far more than peace; this woman was joy personified.

She was also an inmate at a federal correctional institute.

My twenty-eight-year-old self had never thought to even imagine the inside of a prison. Security was tight as we walked into that prison: cameras visible in every corner, guards stationed and watchful, and more scanners available than NYC's JFK International Airport. The small group of women from my church emptied our pockets and left our belongings with a heavily armed gentleman at the first scanner, and then another guard led us into a brightly lit gymnasium full of sixty women in khaki jumpsuits. We were there to sing carols and share the hopeful message of Christmas.

Or so we thought.

One tall, curly-haired woman smiled at us from the front of the room. She welcomed us forward, excitedly introducing us as we walked to the front. She was clearly in charge, and the women in the room knew it. You could feel their respect emanating with each word she spoke. I couldn't help but feel it, too. This woman commanded respect with a charismatic energy that was palpable.

We spent an hour celebrating Christmas with them, singing songs and sharing stories of faith. They raised their hands, closed their eyes, and held each other. They laughed and cried. The tears reminded us of the depth of pain held within those walls; yet that pain clearly coexisted with joy, sharing the same space, as it often does.

That evening, I spoke to the group of women about the simplicity and beauty of the first Christmas and the things in our modern celebrations that get in the way of experiencing it. Many of these things these women had left behind when they began life behind bars. Yet here I was in a prison witnessing a joy that none of us expected to find—and maybe hadn't found ourselves that holiday, until then. I told the women incarcerated there that for the first time that season, there in that room, I felt the spirit of Christmas, pure and free.

After the program, we spent time talking together. These women were, in many ways, like us. They had children and families in the outside world. They missed their kids and wanted a better life for them. They loved them from afar. Many found themselves in situations they never dreamed they would be in: one bad decision or one wrong relationship had sealed their fate. In this room they were allowed to be human: accepted, loved, and valued.

Before I left, I wanted to thank the tall woman who welcomed us and led the event. I gave her a hug and held both of her hands in mine. She was a confident leader and looked so happy and ready to take on the world. *She must be getting out of here soon*, I thought.

So, I said to her, "You are just amazing. How much time do you have left here?"

She paused and smiled peacefully as she looked me in the eyes. With a nod of her head, she replied.

"I have life."

Those words, her smile, her peace, and her joy: these have returned to me countless times over the last twenty years. In moments of frustration, when I am searching for contentment, I remember this beautiful spiritual teacher who showed me, in just a few moments, that contentment is a learned practice. It can be found in *any* circumstance. We just need to look for it in the right places.

Fast forward to today. As I mentioned at the start of this book, I often wrote these chapters on days I had a heavy heart. Today was one of them. It's spring right now where I live, and it was warm enough today to sit outside on my patio this morning with my laptop and a cup of coffee. I didn't sleep much last night because my thoughts were racing from one stressor to another.

A few minutes ago, my sister Krissy called to check on me. I answered from my perch on my back patio.

"How are you—wait, and *where* are you? And what is that sound?" she asked me.

I stopped for a moment and listened. Until my sister mentioned it, I hadn't even noticed any sounds. But surrounding me was a symphony of birdsong, filling the air in my backyard. Although I couldn't see them, in the trees, there were a multitude of birds, singing and calling to each other sweetly and melodically. Once she pointed out the sounds, I couldn't believe I hadn't heard it, as it was so loud!

I took a few deep breaths with my eyes closed. I sat in the center of the songs, listening to them swirl around me. They enveloped me and carried me to another place. For the first time in twenty-four hours, my anxious nerves began to settle.

I wonder how that amazing woman found contentment in prison. What does she do? I imagine she isn't always content, and that she, too, struggles to maintain her joy in the most difficult of circumstances. But she clearly knew a depth of joy that many of us can only aspire to.

I took another look up at the trees, this time fully aware of the songs that surrounded me. A wave of calm slowly washed over me. Contentment. If you look in the right places, you will most certainly find it. You may even begin to see that it's all around you.

Soul-Full Season: In what circumstance might God be calling you to learn contentment? Where in your circumstance, if nothing changes, might you find it?

Baby, Stay Calm Inside:
- What brings you contentment this season? What makes it hard to find?
- Write down some of those things. Sit with that list each morning as an intentional practice to remind you of the things most important to you before you begin your day.

15

Connected and Content

EVERY YEAR I look forward to the white elephant gift exchange I do with seven of my girlfriends. If you are unfamiliar with this game, here's a quick synopsis: everyone brings a wrapped gift. Ours usually reflect a different theme each year, like self-care or a guilty pleasure. Each person draws a number, and the person with the number one opens a gift first. Number two can steal that gift or choose to open a new one. Number three can steal either of the gifts or can choose one for herself, and so on.

When someone decides to stop playing nice and steal a coveted gift, it's game on! No longer are we well-behaved adults; our inner kids emerge, and we simply want what we want. We don't only laugh at each other's reactions; sometimes, a gift itself is pretty bizarre and usually reflective of the friend who brought it. (To those seven friends: you know what and who I'm referring to.) These are evenings of joyful connection.

When I was writing a book on the eight keys to contentment, people frequently asked me, "But what is *the* key to contentment—if you had to pick just one?" This is a hard question, and I don't like to answer it. The eight keys to contentment that I wrote about work synergistically, and each one matters.

There is something to be said, however, for the life-giving power of connection.

As we get older, we often don't realize how much we need meaningful, social connection. *Meaningful* is the key. Maybe because we are so tired from packed schedules, running from one commitment to another—work to kids to dinner to bed and then repeat—that it's easier to *not* connect with others. In fact, I think many of us are trying to intentionally *disconnect* in order to find a little head space and increase our mental bandwidth.

We can certainly keep up with our friends' lives through Instagram stories, which offer a type of pseudo-connection by way of clever one-liners and colorful emojis. Yet there's nothing like an evening in the company of friends to help you ignite the spark of real-life human connection.

Every time I experience a meaningful connection, no matter how small, a little ember within me lights up and comes alive. It could be simple moments, like asking about someone's ailing mother or sharing a kid-friendly recipe. It happens in sideline conversations on a sports field, when another parent shares a story about their struggling teen and reassures me that mine is not alone. Misery loves company, so I also think of the many conversations I have had about the maelstrom of perimenopause, in which we agree that "no, we are not crazy" and that "yes, we feel crazy." I think about these moments well after they are over.

We were literally designed for connection. Our body, mind, and spirit function optimally when we have close, connected relationships. The longest study on well-being, the Harvard Study of Adult Development, is an eighty-five-year-old continuing study revealing what it takes to lead a happy and healthy life. According to the comprehensive data, love makes more of a difference than IQ, social status, or genetics when it comes to longevity and fulfillment.

We can even quantify just how much of a difference it makes. One finding in the study revealed that a person's overall relationship satisfaction at age *fifty* proved to be a better predictor of physical health at age *eighty* than cholesterol scores. Connected relationships minimize the perception of physical pain. The study revealed that those now in their eighties who have had happy marriages reported that their moods did not suffer even when in physical pain. Conversely, those who did not have happy marriages experienced more emotional and physical pain than those who did.

In 2023, Surgeon General Vivek Murthy declared a public health crisis of loneliness, which is now considered a significant health risk. Not only does loneliness impact mental health, increasing the likelihood of depression by 50 percent, but people who are lonely also experience a 29 percent increase in heart disease, 32 percent risk of stroke, 50 percent risk of developing dementia, and a 60 percent risk of premature death.

These numbers speak for themselves. Connection protects us, fulfills us, and keeps us alive.

During the holidays, though, meaningful connection with others is what we often lack. When we are so occupied with doing and decorating, buying and baking, we don't have the time (let alone the energy) for real connection. When I actually do have conversations at a gathering or event this time of year, my mind is often like a game of ping-pong, constantly bouncing back to what I have left to do or how much I would love to just curl up in my bed and go to sleep. Yet because connection *is* the essence of this season for me, I now find myself often repeating this reminder to help me quickly find perspective: connection over perfection. It's amazing how quickly I am able to let go of less important things when I keep those three words in mind.

Embrace connection over perfection.

We can choose specific moments during the holidays to go slower and focus on connection over perfection. Perhaps we have to simplify life where we can, to be more present. For example, set out platters for an event rather than prepare an elaborate meal to be able to enjoy the company of others instead of fussing over food. Sometimes, we have to create moments for connection that we actually look forward to because, let's be honest, not all holiday interactions are enjoyable. (More on that later.)

What do you do for fun? Yes, you. I'm asking you, the person who makes sure everyone else is enjoying themselves. *You.* I can't even tell you how many times I have asked this question to a grown woman during a therapy session, and she sits there in silence. "Having a drink with friends" is a common answer. That might certainly be a moment of connection, but I think we can do better when it comes to uninhibited, exhilarating fun like we had as teenagers. Hard to remember, right? But when we pair connection with fun, we level up to joy.

For me, that white elephant evening with friends that I host each year epitomizes my kind of fun and meaningful connection. Not only do I feel that little ember within aglow, but I also usually laugh so hard I've either cried or peed (likely both). Interwoven throughout the night are also moving conversations, some that even bring tears. These are the ones that arise when you feel comfortable enough to be your true self. Vulnerability—when you can open yourself up and be seen for who you are by another—is the beating heart of connection.

Your connection does not have to be found at a gathering or a party. It may be an intimate hike with a loved one after a fresh snowfall. Perhaps it's finally scheduling the coffee with a friend who you always say you will see but never do.

Whatever it is, take the time and make the time for it this season. The call, the walk, the coffee when it's meaningful, it is *always* worth it.

Baby, Stay Calm Inside:
- Can you find a moment for connection and fun on your terms this season—maybe even one out of your comfort zone?
- The first step is to actually think about what could be fun for you. Maybe it's glow-in-the-dark tobogganing, a bonfire, or a night walk through a brightly lit city after catching a show with a friend.
- This season, write down the moments when you experience connection. This will make you more aware of them as they happen. Go back at the end of the holiday season and read them to hold on to joy after the season ends.

16

Holiday Drama 101

MAYBE YOU'RE A person who can handle the stress of the holidays just fine and still find delight. You find moments of meaningful connection even in this busy season, and you practice gratitude all day long. But for many of us, the holidays are extra hard for one reason: drama.

If so, this is the moment you have been waiting for. We've come to the topic at the root of why you might need a therapist to talk you through the holidays in the first place.

When you are forced to be with certain people, the moments of tension and discomfort that emerge threaten to ruin your mood. And it happens like clockwork, year after year. No one wants to deal with drama this time of year, but this is often when it comes to the surface. It may be the funcle who turns into the drunkle or the drama comin' from your mama. Or your loved one's problem that suddenly now, in the close quarters of your family reunion or long travel day, becomes *your* situation.

Whatever the case—whether it's about politics, religion, money, bad memories, or previous arguments—holiday drama is as old as humanity. Relationship drama is my most requested topic to speak on when it comes to the holidays. So, know that you are not alone.

The good news is that we don't have to get our tinsel in a tangle. This chapter and the next one contain my top tips to keep your calm and carry on your merry way.

First, *center yourself.* It's always wise to start with ourselves because that is the only person we can truly control. When facing holiday drama, ask yourself, What part of this can I control, and what part can I not? I like to take notes on control in two columns: "what I can't control" and "what I can control." Then I focus on the actions on that list because that is really all I can change. Writing it down makes it visual and very clear.

Here are some of the things I have written in the past within my control when faced with holiday conflict. I can

> breathe to calm down.
> leave the room or walk away.
> remind myself of what is good.
> laugh.
> extend kindness and empathy.
> try to see it from their perspective, even if I don't agree.
> stay surface and don't take the bait.
> change the subject.
> hold on to the big-picture perspective: this too shall pass.

Some of these actions I will discuss more in chapter twenty, which is about managing holiday anxiety. The rest we will discuss in chapter seventeen. For now, here's one more strategy.

Pregame: Plan ahead and prepare yourself for the drama. I'm not talking about alcohol here—although a little spiked eggnog for some could be helpful (and when I say some, I mean me). I am referring to getting ahead of any possible known conflict. Years from now, you don't want a conflict to be the most memorable part of the holiday, which it could be ("Remember when Auntie Sonia poured the gravy on Uncle Junior's head?").

If you have known these characters your whole life, likely the drama is not new. It may be present in new situations, but it's likely that the underlying issues have been around for quite some time.

What I'm trying to say is this: if you have had these issues for twenty years, this holiday is not the time to solve them.

I wish most people wanted a conflict-free holiday, but unfortunately that's just not true. Some people thrive on conflict, and they make sure to instigate it. They like to provoke a reaction.

If you would like to enjoy the holidays with as little conflict as possible, it's worth having a conversation or sending a message beforehand, asking to keep the conflictual topic aside for the time you are together. You could text or email or call the other person with a simple message: "Hey, I know there has been a lot between us. I'm sure you want to enjoy the holiday, and I do too, so let's not talk about *x* when you come over. Is it okay if we just focus on having a peaceful holiday (and address our issue later)?"

If there is something that needs to be discussed, consider meeting to discuss it beforehand. Or set a date to meet *after* the holidays to talk and work things out.

Every situation is different, and these suggestions may not be right for every situation. If the holiday drama in your house is so distressing that you find yourself shutting down, withdrawing, or constantly seething with anger, it is absolutely worth reaching out to a therapist to help navigate it.

Baby, Stay Calm Inside:
- What can you do to calm yourself in the face of conflict?
- Is there a particular situation that you may need to use this technique in?
- What could be helpful to keep in mind so you can extend a little grace to someone who is hard to handle during the holidays?

17

The Three Ds of Holiday Conflict

CONGRATULATIONS: YOU'VE NOW passed Holiday Drama 101! You know how to center yourself, and you've done what you can to pregame it. You've prepared yourself for the conflict that may arise, and maybe you've even reached out to the other person to decide together how to approach potential conflicts.

But in some relationships, healthy conversations are just not possible. You've tried before but never got anywhere. In those cases, as you anticipate holiday time with family and friends, think of the strategies in this chapter. Remember: you can't control how another person will respond. But all these strategies *are* within your control: deflect, declare, and depersonalize.

Deflect: *Change the subject.* You might be accustomed to viewing deflection as a negative strategy. But depending on the argument and the context, changing the subject might be just the thing to bring calm to the situation.

Have a few lines ready to change the subject when tense topics come up:

"Who's excited to get socks for Hannukah this year?"
"Did I tell you how beautiful the fourth-grade winter concert was? It made me teary!"
"What is everyone wearing for Diwali?"
"I wonder if Santa will put underwear in the stockings again."
"Anyone want seconds? Can I get anyone a drink?"
"I'm going to help Dad out in the kitchen."

Find something you are comfortable with and keep it on hand for when you need it.

Laughter can also be a deflection. Have a funny joke in mind, think of something comedic that someone said or did, or recall a hilarious story from a past holiday and share it. Laughing is part of a therapeutic intervention in dialectical behavioral therapy called *opposite action*, which encourages doing exactly the opposite of how you feel. Smiling or laughing can get us unstuck in these moments, and it also helps us to reclaim the power. You can do it privately or publicly in the moment. It will certainly lighten the mood and your spirits.

Randomly laugh out loud, and don't even worry about explaining it; just keep them guessing. When in doubt, drop a passing, "Oh nothing, I was just thinking about something that happened earlier today." Then exit stage left.

The gold standard when it comes to minimizing holiday drama is boundaries. These are not your typical request-type boundaries. These are the ones you boldly . . .

Declare: *Create holiday boundaries.* Often when people begin setting boundaries, they still give the power to the person who will violate the boundaries.

What do I mean by this? Here are a few examples:

"Please don't talk about your political views at dinner."
"I'd like you not to mention the divorce in front of the kids."
"I'm busy on Wednesday. Can you come visit on Friday instead?"
"Please don't invite my ex to the holiday party."

These aren't boundaries; these are requests. If someone doesn't honor a boundary that you set, what are you going to do about it? A strong boundary should make that piece clear.

Try using "if-then" statements when thinking about your boundaries. Try declaring them boldly:

"If you bring up politics, I will leave the table, and sadly we won't be able to spend the holidays together in the future."
"If you talk about the divorce in front of the kids, I will change the subject and ask you to leave."
"We would love to see you, and if you would like to come visit, Friday works for us."
"If you bring my ex to the holiday party, you both will eat outside on the deck." (Not a great option for winter in Connecticut.)

Do you see the difference between a boundary request and an actual boundary? We are not asking; we are telling.

Setting a boundary in this way may feel like a bold step for you, especially if you have had weak boundaries in the past. It might feel uncomfortable. But just think about what has happened when you *haven't* had strong boundaries. It's worth a try if it can protect your peace or even the peace of those around you.

One last reminder: "No" is a boundary and a complete sentence. Saying no opens doors to more fulfilling experiences you want to focus on this holiday. So, saying no to the holiday party with people you don't want to see makes saying *yes* to watching holiday movies on the couch while curling up with your dog possible.

Depersonalize: *It's not about you!* This is the season of good tidings, right?

"God bless us, every one!" Tiny Tim reminds us.

But not everyone has been blessed in the same ways, and the resulting wounds go deep. There are so many situations in which, sadly, you may simply be collateral damage. There is truth to the saying "Hurt people hurt people." The issue may come *at* you, but it likely isn't *about* you.

> **There are so many situations in which, sadly, you may simply be collateral damage. The issue may come *at* you, but it likely isn't *about* you.**

So how do we get to a place of compassion? I often ask myself these questions both when I am working with a client and when I am dealing with a tough person in my own life:

> What has happened in this person's life that has made them act in this way?
> How has this person been hurt in the past or present?
> What is the underlying need here that is coming to the surface right now—and what are the roots of this need? Where did it start?

These questions help to access the bigger picture that can help you see the wounds that likely don't have much to do with you. They also can help you extend some compassion during this season—or at least help you to disengage from the conflict.

Keep in mind that the holidays can be very difficult and painful for some people because of past trauma. If you have kids, this is also a great opportunity to model healthy responses in conflict. Believe me: they are watching, and those patterns will be repeated.

Holding your response for a moment, taking a breath, focusing on what is good in your own life, and setting a boundary during the holidays might be the best things you can do. Deflect, declare a boundary, and depersonalize: these three actions can carry us through.

I'm not suggesting that we repress difficult conversations or conflict forever. Still, a silent night this time of year can preserve some peace when we need it most.

Baby, Stay Calm Inside:
- What is one boundary you need to set this holiday to preserve your peace or the peace of those around you?
- Who can help you hold this boundary or remind you of it?
- What conflict is not worth addressing this year?

18

Is Less Really More?

YOU KNOW BY now that my husband and I are Christmas Eve wrappers. Every year I say, "We are never doing this again." But, sure enough, history repeats itself. Yes, we have had one-off years, years where we were not up until the wee hours of the morning. But that is not our norm.

Our ritual of procrastination gives all my type A friends anxiety just reading about it—you know, the people who are wrapping presents as our leaves here in New England begin to turn color. It actually gives me anxiety, too. Because at the culmination of the most labor-intensive season—after an evening Christmas Eve service and a festive dinner with the entire family—I know what awaits.

Around 10:30 p.m., we begin to drag out the boxes: unopened Amazon boxes, that is. In the weeks leading up to Christmas, I don't even bother opening all of them. I just hide them when they arrive, not really knowing what's inside and hoping that whatever I have ordered came. We begin the unboxing, and every year my husband makes the same comments: "What's with all of this stuff? Do they need all of this? Every year you say we will do less—and every year it seems like there is even more!"

I nod and agree. He's not wrong. I always begin with good intentions, starting a list on my Notes app to try to keep track of who gets what and how much we are spending on each kid. Yet, a few trips to Target and some late-night browsing online ("She would just *love* this . . .") can quickly spin out of control.

Yes, I'm the woman who writes about contentment not being about *stuff*! Yet, from what I know, I am not alone here. This idea of being satisfied with less, especially during the holidays, is foreign to many. Stress and money go hand in hand, and overspending can be a large part of holiday stress.

Holiday spending can also lead to pervasive stress year-round, which affects our physical and mental health and relationships. *Forbes Advisor* reported in a 2023 survey that 36 percent of people anticipated spending more that year than in previous years, with only 13 percent expecting to spend less. More than 50 percent of respondents chose to pay by credit card, and 42 percent of those people expected to accumulate $500 or more in credit card debt. Some 33 percent of respondents planned to use, instead of credit cards, the "buy now, pay later" options.

"The January you really resents the December you," is how financial expert and *New York Times*–bestselling author Rachel Cruze puts it. "Emotions rise up, and it's important to be tethered to something, especially when it comes to money.

Have a plan before the emotions get crazy and the events start, and the January you will love the December you."

I've been impressed by Rachel's wisdom when it comes to financial matters and the psychology behind spending. Her podcast, *The Rachel Cruze Show*, is a wealth of information, and I knew I had to sit down with her to hear her perspective on all things holiday.

In both of our fields—psychology and finance—Rachel and I have seen how the stories we tell ourselves, which originate in the families we grew up in, shape how we approach the holidays. Because families are so different, this can cause conflict around beliefs about spending.

"You may want a big Christmas, but why?" Rachel asks. She stresses the importance of asking the questions that lead to our deeper motivations. "Maybe you are coming out of a place where you didn't have much, and now want to do better," she says. Conversely, she also sees people influenced by a scarcity mindset for the same reason: when you are "always focused on saving," you can have "a hard time letting go" and enjoying life.

Rachel encourages people to talk to their spouses about holiday spending. If you are not the primary earner in the family, perhaps your partner is carrying that stress. "Talk about it *before* the holidays," she says. "Ask why we want what we want. When we can start talking about those parts of our hearts and those motivations, the layers under 'I just want to buy that for the kids,' we are getting somewhere."

Rachel encourages us to try to understand where the other person is coming from and "lead with empathy. Say, 'I totally get that for you. How can we get that same feeling without overspending?' You want to be on the same team."

Rachel has three young kids of her own, alongside a successful career, and I asked her how she keeps track of spending during the holidays. Rachel says she tries to make things visual. Write down the budget. "As much as you can, have it visual and not in your head. You will make better decisions," she says. This tracks with research that reports that keeping lists going in your head, rather than on paper, can lead to you feeling overwhelmed. On her Notes app, Rachel lists out each kid and what they want with pricing to keep track. She says both kids and adults get excited, and with the emotion of the holiday, many people can forget about any budget. "But be the adult in this scenario!" she says.

We talked about research that points to happiness not being about bigger, better, and more, and about how dopamine attached to these new, material things eventually disappears. Rachel encourages her clients to rely on those experts. "Experiences bring a higher level of joy than material things. Say, 'Let's try it and if you hate it, we can go back.' It's worth trying something new and getting out of the rat race of comparison. Christmas is magnified and exhausting."

With many families struggling financially around the holidays, Rachel says it's so important to set expectations. "Depending on what's going on with your family that year, it's important to have conversations."

It's true that a holiday can look different with new limitations if you are facing job loss, divorce, grief, or illness. We both agree it's so important to talk to kids about how things might be different. I loved how Rachel phrased such conversations as "share, don't scare." Kids likely know something is going on and need some level of information about changed circumstances in your household; they also still need parental reassurance that things will be okay and that they still can have a happy holiday. She suggests simple, short conversations, such as saying, "Hey, this is probably going to look a little different this year, but we are still going to have fun . . . and there will be some surprises!"

Personally, I'm now going to start asking myself, "What does January me think about this?" Getting to the core of what you want for the holiday, and why, is central to having a connected, meaningful one.

And once you do, please, take it from me: wrap early and often.

Baby, Stay Calm Inside:
- Is overspending an issue for you that creates stress? What is the motivation behind the spending?
- Are there any experiences you would consider for you or your family in place of gifts?
- What could you do differently this year that might help the January you to feel calmer?

19

The Empty Seat

YOU KNOW HOW you have that one friend who *is* the holidays? The one who lives and breathes the holiday and who shares their joy with anyone in a four-mile radius? This is my friend Gabbie.

I remember attending one of her glamorous holiday parties years ago, an annual event that her friends looked forward to each December. Ed and I were new on the guest list that year. Gabbie transformed her home into a magical winter wonderland. Each room boasted an elegant Christmas tree beautifully decorated by Gabbie herself, with its own whimsical colors and themes. The food was exquisite, as Gabbie had created each delectable mini dessert and ten different kinds of frosted Christmas cookies. In the center of the great room, stood a sparkling eighteen-foot tree dressed in silver and white.

Yet even this stunner could not compete with the life of the party: Gabbie's ugly-sweater-vest–dressed husband, Pepper.

I will never forget watching Pepper that evening, in the center of their dance floor surrounded by friends. The DJ was blasting hip-hop, and this 6'1" white boy was showing off his moves, which were pretty impressive. I leaned over and whispered to my husband, "That guy grew up with Brown and Black people."

One thing was for certain: both Pepper's and Gabbie's joy were contagious. Everyone felt it and their love for one another.

All of that changed literally overnight.

Pepper died in a car accident in 2021, leaving behind Gabbie and her three kids, ages seven, twelve, and thirteen at the time. Since then, holidays have been different for her and her family. I sat down with her to ask her how she navigates them now. As someone who has always adored Christmas, how does she cope with grief and loss during the holidays?

"Christmas was all about tradition," she tells me. "My mom instilled a love of Christmas in me when I was growing up. Every surface of the house was decorated, and we dressed up and had a fancy dinner. Later, I enjoyed the process of making the house come alive with joy and celebration. But the first year after losing Pepper—I didn't want a holiday. I didn't have the motivation to decorate. I didn't want to make my beautiful table and see the empty seat."

Gabbie decided to travel to Puerto Rico to celebrate that first Christmas with her kids and extended family. She knew she needed to be out of their house that year and away from those memories. "It's okay to change locations and traditions, and to give yourself grace to celebrate the holiday without it being exactly how it was," she tells me. "Some traditions might be too painful." She also suggests surrounding yourself with people who you can be honest with about what you want to do and don't on that day.

Gabbie's kids have been her motivation to keep the holidays festive. "I didn't want Christmas to have left me because of grief. I can find joy through my kids. I'm so thankful for their strength. They never have used the loss as an excuse to not show up or do their best, so I, too, had to show up for them. I couldn't say to my kids, 'We're not doing Christmas this year.'"

Four years have passed since their father's death, and Gabbie once again tries to keep as many of their traditions as possible, especially those that celebrate their dad. Each year they make Pepper's favorite pie and talk about the poem he wrote before they whisked them off to Disney World for a holiday vacation. They take out the photo of mommy kissing "Santa Claus" in the living room while the kids were asleep. Gabbie admits it's hard as a single mom to create this whole magical experience on her own every year, but she has learned to give herself grace.

"I take it year by year. I make time for exercise, and I read instead of scroll. I also have learned to be more open with my gratitude. It's a practice I needed to learn. Although my life has been challenged, in some crazy way I am grateful for it. It taught me how strong I am and what I am capable of. My gratitude practice is often before I go to bed: I will say, 'I am thankful for my three healthy kids, for my mom, for my health.' I want to be focused on what is positive because then that's what you will attract."

That first holiday after Pepper's death, I went to Gabbie's home. It was beautifully decorated, but it was different than before; it felt light, airy, and ethereal. Gabbie told me she had help from her friend Molly, a talented interior designer who knew the family well and who had also lost her own father when she was very young.

"I offered," Molly told me when I spoke to her. "I asked her, 'Can I help you? Would you like some help?' Gabbie is a great mom, and I knew she wanted to keep things fun for the kids. We changed it up, kept some familiar things and left some out. The important thing is to meet that person where they are at. It's therapeutic to know you can still do some of these things and it doesn't have to be the same."

Gabbie appreciated that Molly asked her what she could do, and Gabby now encourages others to ask those who are grieving this time of year what you can do to help. "Don't try to talk them into anything. Just ask what makes them feel comfortable and will allow them to get through the day. Do they want to do more or less? How would they like to celebrate? If they verbalize it, do your best to support that, even if it's not what *you* want for them. If they don't know, just shower them with love and support and check on them often."

I have often told people that doing or saying nothing for fear of upsetting the person is usually worse. Gabbie agrees. "It's not okay to say nothing. A simple, 'I'm so sorry you are going through this. Is there anything I can do?' is good. It's not rocket science. You don't have to be a therapist, just a human being with a heart."

Since Pepper died, Gabbie has felt his presence in many ways and at important transitions in her life. One of them included buying her new home, which happened to be a house for sale right next to the home of one of her best friends. Selling their family home with their memories of Pepper was a big decision and one that Gabbie felt unsure about. On her first visit to the prospective new house, directly in front of the sidewalk, she noticed a little white packet that said "Pepper." Confirmation? I believe it and so does Gabbie.

That new home has brought her much joy and a new beginning in many ways. I often remind my beautiful, tall, blonde friend that it's her "Barbie dream house," and each room reflects her style and personality. Gabbie says, "Getting to decorate this home was new and exciting and gave me the freedom to enjoy the holidays in a new way. I like to be surrounded by people because my grief is the loudest when I am alone. I now enjoy entertaining people at my home and celebrating the holiday well before the actual day, which is less emotionally triggering."

We are sitting in her colorfully elegant living room with pops of hot pink when, toward the end of our conversation, the lights in her house flicker.

"Hmm. That's never happened before," she says, looking around.

I have a feeling I know who is responsible for the interruption.

"He just can't mind his own business! Yes, we are talking about you!" I say, looking up. We both laugh.

"One more thing," Gabbie adds, in terms of advice to other grievers during the holiday. "Don't feel guilty to laugh, smile, and sing carols with friends and family . . . They would want you to be happy. They would want you to celebrate."

Baby, Stay Calm Inside:
- If you are grieving, what do you need to make this holiday manageable for you?
- Do you need to ask for help? If so, who do you know who would love to help you?
- If you know someone grieving, ask what you can do to make this holiday better for them. Perhaps extend an invite to your holiday table. This simple gesture will not be forgotten.

20

A Perspective on Pain

DOES YOUR HOLIDAY stress consist of the possibility that you may not get your six bathrooms renovated in time for your guests' arrival? Is there a delay on your imported porcelain tile from Italy, so you might not have Christmas with the family in your dream kitchen? If so, please don't come talk to me.

I'm serious: don't tell me about it.

I retired from therapy in a wealthy area for several years because I couldn't find genuine empathy for these stories anymore and had a hard time looking below the surface. (It's true that I was also burned-out with my own life stressors, not my clients' fault. In my humble opinion, no empathy means game over for a therapist. Take a break. Don't offer therapy to others until you can get it back.)

Therapists often try to normalize pain for everyone, as we should. Yes, it is true that each of us has different thresholds for stress and varying degrees of resilience, depending on our life experiences and personalities. Stress is certainly relative. For that reason, most therapists will say, "There is no hierarchy of pain," or "You can't rank stress."

I do believe this to be true. Your pain is relative to your life experiences and ability to cope with stress in a given moment, which can be negatively impacted by other stressors in your life. Maybe something that's not a big deal becomes a big deal because a family member is ill or you've just gone through a break up. However, it's important to be able to recognize this. If we can't, on some level, recognize the distinctions between different kinds of stress—say, between imported tile on back order versus a serious illness—we have lost a fundamental human compass: perspective.

Listen (honestly, no judgment): you can't help how you feel when your six bathrooms aren't getting renovated. I personally know many beautiful people who get caught up in this kind of stress and lose perspective. You feel real psychological and physiological symptoms from this, and yes, those things are real.

Just be cognizant about who you share that kind of stress with this time of year. *I* won't judge you, but I promise many will, silently, while nodding and looking sympathetic. The good news is that some of the techniques that I discuss in the next chapter will help you. (Sidebar: this specific type of seemingly superficial stress always goes deeper than it appears. It often originates with a core belief that sounds like "I'm not enough" and surfaces in many unexpected ways. There is work to be done to uncover what the underlying matter is. If this is you that I'm talking about, please talk to someone who can help because it tends to not go away until you do the work.)

Now, back to the rest of you: those of you constantly battling an emotional blizzard whirling around you with gale-force winds; who are reliving grief or trauma; who don't know how you are going to provide gifts for your kids; who are facing a life-altering family, career, or health situation. Back to those of you who consider it a win to just get out of bed in the mornings: I'm not about to minimize your pain with a few prescriptive techniques, nor can I promise to make it better.

Your pain is next-level, and this time of year may open old wounds and throw salt on new ones. You are in the season of taking things one day at a time or even one hour at a time. You need your people, you need support, and you need your faith or the faith of those who believe that this too shall pass and can see your future beyond this. Hold on to those people and those things tightly, with clenched fists, and don't let go. Know you are the very people I wrote this book for during my own season of ongoing crisis. I have said prayers for you, prayers I have tucked into the pages of these chapters, so that you might feel there is hope ahead. I hope you feel that now.

I would give anything to wave a therapeutic wand and make your pain disappear. I can't. What I *can* do is offer some direction to help manage the moments that feel very intense. Remember: this book is not a substitute for your own therapy or personal connections, which are vital in this season. But it is a starting place, and a reminder that there are things you can still do, even in the fiercest of storms.

Lastly, all my perimenopausal ladies in the house, put your hands up. Anxiety and panic due to estrogen decline, along with a host of other symptoms, are real. Perimenopause will make this time of year even harder, with the increase in cortisol due to all the holiday stress factors, lack of sleep, and exponential increase in responsibilities for many women. I won't get into the research here, but if you are in this age range and experiencing other symptoms consistent with perimenopause, please educate yourself and advocate for yourself with your doctor. If you are practicing the techniques in this book yet still not feeling like yourself, consider asking your doctor about treating estrogen decline before trying or changing a psychotropic medication.

In a world where we often confuse tile delays with trauma, perspective is priceless. In short, don't stress when you don't need to.

Baby, Stay Calm Inside:
- Is there any stressor in your life that just isn't worth stressing over?
- For those of you who are dealing with deep pain, take one day at a time. What do you need today?

21

The Holiday A-List (A Is for Anxiety)

LET IT GO: if only it was as easy as ice queen Elsa made it sound in *Frozen*. But most of us who struggle with anxiety know that letting it go is not so simple. Plus, since we tend to get less sleep during the holidays and have more to do, our ability to cope with stress decreases even further.

Not only have I worked as an anxiety therapist for nearly two decades, but I've also lived with anxiety for nearly five. This chapter and the next detail things that have made the most difference in helping me keep my anxiety and panic in check. These strategies and research-based tips have also helped my patients get control of their anxiety and resume a more balanced, healthy life.

In college, we had a nightly tradition in the dorms called M&Cs—short for milk and cookies. While it wasn't always cookies, there was always a sweet treat to look forward to, offering a little comfort and a much-needed break from the stress of studying. Now that I no longer have the metabolism of a twenty-year-old, I had to come up with another version of M&Cs to manage my stressors.

So, here are a few M&Cs for dealing with holiday anxiety that will hopefully give you something to look forward to and help to bring down your stress level in this season.

Meditate: When we meditate, or even simply when we maintain a single focus rather than multitasking, we eliminate the low levels of anxiety that result from constant thought switching. The research is plentiful on meditation's ability to change brain regions so that we become less reactive to stress and calmer. I will always encourage formal meditative practices if you have the motivation and can make the time. However, knowing how much you have on your plate right now, I know that informal meditation might be a better option for this time of year.

Informal meditation is essentially single tasking or focusing on one thing and one thing only. As you are doing it, immerse yourself in the five senses. Try making your coffee as you observe the sight, sound, and smell of it. You can take five minutes while eating or driving and completely focus on those acts—without listening to music, talking, or scrolling. What this practice does is train your brain to be present in the moment. Those five minutes, consistently over time, will make a significant difference in helping you to live a more present life.

Anxiety is very much focused on the past and the future, so training your mind to be grounded in the *present* not only calms anxious nerves, but it also moves you away from the places anxiety likes best.

Connect: I've written a whole chapter on connection, so you know the importance of it. Simply put, it helps to talk to a kind human, either about what's going on or about other things to distract you from it. I'm a big fan of the "walk and talk" with a friend, which I began to incorporate regularly in my schedule when I started to have panic attacks. This time of year, consistency can be hard, but convince your friend that she needs a break, too. Walking will also allow you to indulge a bit more in those holiday treats without the guilt. Even once a week for thirty minutes can make a difference in letting go of some of the stress.

Move: Research has proven that consistent exercise is a mood elevator and an effective preventative measure for both depression and anxiety for *everyone*. Without fail, when clients incorporate exercise into their daily lives, I have seen their energy levels, self-esteem, and outlook on life improve. Even a twenty-minute daily break to move will make a difference if you are feeling anxious.

Control the Right Column: We often perseverate on what we can't control. If you are reading these chapters in order so far, you have read about the two-column technique: writing down what I can control and what I cannot control. See what you wrote in that second column? Guess what? You can't do anything about that! No matter how much you think about it or talk about it, it won't make a difference; in fact, anxiety can worsen as our brains create stronger neural pathways around those intrusive and repetitive thoughts.

So, let's direct all of that wasted energy into something more effective: the first column. What can you do to make changes to alleviate anxiety within *that* column? What is one thing you can do? One boundary you can set? When we ask these questions, we stretch our cognitive capacity, which becomes impaired when we feel anxious. Asking these specific questions can point to the answers we need. In all my years of doing therapy, I have never had a client not find at least one answer. Usually we know what to do; we just need to do it.

Medicate When Needed: One thing I know for sure is that medication, when needed, is a game changer. I have seen countless patients' lives changed by the right medication at the right time. For myself and one of my children, it was one tool in a toolbox of strategies that helped to move the needle of anxiety. For many people, anxiety is so high, and our nervous systems are so dysregulated, that therapeutic tools alone aren't as effective, or it takes a lot longer to see progress. Medication can offer a reset to the system and a little boost so that the work you do becomes fruitful. One more note: medication should always be monitored by a physician and accompanied by life-changing habits and strategies to help lower anxiety and manage stress long term.

Count on the Cold: Anxiety and panic result from an overactive or dysregulated sympathetic nervous system. That mental red panic button has been hit one too many times, and now it is easily set off or even stuck, sending you frequently into fight, flight, or freeze mode to mediate the perceived threat.

There are several ways to activate our parasympathetic nervous system (PNS), which can help to counter this response. Exposure to cold is one of them.

Panic can happen out of seemingly nowhere, especially if there is a good deal of internalized, unattended-to stress. It's my body's way of sending me a much-needed "code red" message. The body speaks loudly, doesn't it? Panic is one way it says, "There is something wrong that needs attention now."

The debilitating symptoms of panic can be addressed before we even know what's causing it. Panic or severe anxiety can present as nausea, dizziness, heart palpitations, a feeling like you can't breathe, or my personal favorite: a feeling like you are crawling out of your own skin. (If you know, you know.)

When I treat patients who experience panic attacks, cold is a go-to strategy. Placing an ice pack on your head, neck, chest, or pulse points can help to lower these feelings and "turn on" your PNS. Stick your face in a sink full of cold or ice water, take a cold shower, or walk outside in the winter weather in light clothing. Take a cup or water bottle full of ice with you in anxiety-producing situations—planes, for example, for holiday travel. Use ice to alleviate symptoms, too. Even an ice-cold glass of water has been helpful to many of my patients experiencing acute anxiety.

Baby, Stay Calm Inside:
- Which of these strategies could you try today? Even if you don't regularly live with anxiety, you may find these strategies useful to reset when stressed.
- Pick one M&C and practice it through this holiday season. Note how you feel after each week.

22

A Reset for the Season

WHO DOESN'T NEED a reset somewhere in the winter holiday season? We are all going to face situations where we need to take deep breaths at some point. Let's keep going with holiday anxiety management. Here are a few more ideas for things to do when anxiety or panic begins to take over.

And to remind you that you can *reset* in this *season*, this time I have chosen techniques that begin with the letters *r* and *s*.

Respire: In other words, breathe. The key to breathing for relaxation is stimulating the vagus nerve, which happens with a deep and long diaphragmatic exhale. Think of it like this: *longer exhalation is the key to relaxation.* That means your belly inflates like a balloon when you inhale and deflates very slowly with the exhale.

> **Longer exhalation is the key to relaxation.**

I do a four-count inhale and an eight-count exhale. Some like a six-count exhale instead. I have also taught many clients a technique called *box breathing*. Picture the sides of a square:

a four-count inhale, a four-count hold, a four-count exhale, and another four-count hold. I can't say enough about how effective this breathing is for anxiety and stress. The key is to practice it often when you are calm, so that when the anxiety hits, your mind and body know what to do.

By the way, Navy SEALs learn box breathing. They would not go into a battle without mental and physical preparation. Think of fighting anxiety as the same. (This exercise is one of the ways I get resistant men on board with relaxation breathing. They know it's their only chance at sharing any iota of a trait with a SEAL.) The beautiful thing is that this breathing exercise truly does work. If it works for Navy SEALs to combat their life-or-death situations, it will certainly make a difference for our holidays!

Rest: Rest is different than sleep. Ideally, you would get seven or eight hours of sleep a night; I will explain why in a moment. I do realize that this is nearly impossible for most people this time of year. Moments of rest scheduled throughout your week can be helpful to make up some of the difference.

Our brains need cognitive rest or down time. These are times when we are not actively focused or concentrating on performing a task. Cognitive rest can be a catnap for one hour or less, so as not to interfere with night sleep. Exercise such as jogging, doing jumping jacks, or taking a walk through a familiar neighborhood also allows for cognitive rest, as these types of activities can be done mindlessly or meditatively.

When we rest, we engage the brain's default mode network (DMN). The DMN is responsible for important functions, such as retrieving memories, increasing creativity by connecting ideas, and making us feel more connected to ourselves and to others. The DMN functions are especially important during the holidays, when we want to hold on to memories and feel more connected. You could also think of DMN as Do Mostly Nothing.

Reflect: Asking the question "What do I need right now or today?" is a good starting point for self-care. This type of reflection can help us identify what we need in the moment to create some balance. Reflection also involves gratitude. I love the question "What is good today?" Finding the good will redirect our minds from the looping anxious thoughts on replay and release mood-elevating neurochemicals to help combat a negative focus.

Suck on Sour: As I mentioned before, anxious thoughts often play on repeat. Sometimes we need something to break that cycle of pervasive negative thinking. Just like getting cold is a strategy, eating extremely sour-tasting things can break that cycle of anxiety. Biting into a lemon or sucking on a tart sour candy can create an immediate thought switch and engage the senses to snap you out of an anxious moment. Although I have recommended this technique for years, I had never tried it. Why I decided to try it for the first time on national TV, I will never know, because the face I made as I took a big bite into a lemon wedge is one you don't want to make on national TV. But trust me: it 100 percent works. You can't think about anything else in that moment!

Sing: Did you know you cannot be anxious and sing at the same time? Singing requires your brain to direct several mental and physiological processes at once, so there is no space for anxious thoughts while you are singing. The long exhale, as you belt out lyrics, also stimulates the vagus nerve, which calms the fight or flight feelings. Not to mention the joy and nostalgia evoked as we recall some of our favorite tunes will help to calm us as well. So, when your in-laws start acting up, it's time for a boisterous rendition of something. In our house, holiday Mariah usually does the trick.

Sleep: I know: telling a parent to sleep enough the weeks leading up to Christmas is like telling a child to donate all their gifts right after opening them. For most, it's just not gonna happen. But if you are experiencing pervasive anxiety or panic attacks, sleep is a nonnegotiable if you want to get better. I know you have a lot to do, but you won't be able to do as much, cope well with stress, or enjoy these moments if you don't get some sleep (not to mention, you won't remember much of any of this because memories are stored as you sleep). If your anxiety is rising, it will likely get worse without sleep.

Regular bedtimes and consistent wake-up times make a difference in creating a routine with predictability for your mind and body. Anxiety is physically and mentally exhausting, so your mind and body are working overtime and need the rest to recuperate. Seven to eight hours a night is recommended; at the very least, try for six.

I hope these strategies are helpful in managing some of the emotional ups and downs of the holidays. Anxiety is treatable even during the holidays.

Baby, Stay Calm Inside:
- As I said, I will never give you a to-do list this time of year. Perhaps pick just one or two from the list above that you think you need and try to practice it this holiday. Even trying one consistently will add more balance and help to calm the anxiety in this season.

23

Unexpected Gifts

THE SHORT STORY "The Gift of the Magi," published by O. Henry in 1905, is the story of a young couple very much in love looking to find the perfect holiday gift for each other. They have each saved as much as possible, yet they find they do not have enough money to buy something as extraordinary as their lover deserves. So to afford a gift, they each sell their most prized possession. Then they buy the gift they have in mind for the other. Each of them sacrifices that which is most precious and valuable to them in order to give a gift that is worthy of the love they feel for the other.

I won't give away any more details of the plot because it is a story worth reading this time of year. But whenever I revisit this timeless tale, I am struck by this couple's desire to express love through sacrificial giving.

We as humans are wired to give our time, resources, or abilities. And giving has impressive neurological benefits. Giving, especially when we personally connect with the recipient, releases the trifecta of mood-elevating neurochemicals:

dopamine, serotonin, and oxytocin. Dopamine is responsible for motivation, new pleasure, and reward, while serotonin is a natural mood booster, creating a sense of happiness and well-being. Oxytocin is the neurochemical we see in mothers and babies when they bond and in people when they are in love. It's no wonder once we give, we often want to do it again.

I mentioned at the start of the book that this past year had been a difficult one for my family. My youngest daughter, Carolina, who is truly fierce in every way, struggled with a common phobia that presents in children: emetophobia, the fear of throwing up or of someone else throwing up. It doesn't sound all that serious, but it often prevents kids from doing things like attending school, playing sports, going to birthday parties, and traveling.

As a result, Carolina began to act timid and fearful in ways I had never seen before. Many of you have experienced how heartbreaking it is to see a version of your child you no longer recognize. You know what it is like to watch your once strong, joyful, and energetic child be paralyzed by moments of anxiety and panic. Most mornings during that time, Carolina would wake up terrified to go to school. We did everything we could to at least get her into the school building, which often took an hour or more. Together, she and I would slowly make our way from the parking lot into the foyer, utilizing my own form of exposure therapy on the fly. And although she was in the building, I don't believe she attended an entire class for months.

Periodically, I would meet with her principal, counselor, and teacher to come up with a support plan. We brainstormed ways to help get her into the building, thinking of ways to motivate her to get to school. Thankfully, this was not their first rodeo with a student with anxiety, and those dedicated educators came up with the brilliant idea that Carolina could help out in other classrooms. That way, even when she was not attending class regularly, she had a purpose for being in the building. They hoped that giving her some authority and responsibility would imbue a sense of agency and a feeling of control—all of which a child can lose when living with anxiety.

So they created special positions for her in school with younger children. In the mornings, before going to her class, she would stop by the first-grade classroom, greet the children, and help them get unpacked and ready for the day. In the middle of the day, she would support kids with disabilities by reading a book or playing a game. Carolina would end her day with a "bus job," which included lining up and leading the kindergartners to the cafeteria to wait for their buses to be called.

Slowly, day by day, Carolina got better. She got out of bed with a little more energy and asked to return to school after therapy appointments to do her bus job. When they saw her, the kindergartners would run up to her to tackle her with hugs. She knew how they felt about her. Many first-grade moms stopped and said to me, "My daughter just adores Carolina!"

By focusing on what she could do for others, which became a regular practice, Carolina moved through a debilitating phobia and regained the physical and mental strength to get back to herself. I learned so much about my daughter during that time. We learned she is incredibly gifted with kids, especially those with disabilities. Her compassion and empathy for them knows no limits. I don't believe we would have ever discovered these things had she not gone through this most challenging time.

Even if this holiday is not what you expected, you still have much to give. Yes, we took care of my daughter during that time with therapy, sleep, connection with friends, and a whole lot of prayer. But even in her weakest and most fearful moments, she still had much to give.

Giving gives us back to ourselves.

What I know now is this: giving gives us back to ourselves.

Soul-Full Season: Are there any hidden gifts in this unexpected situation you are going through? Have there been hidden gifts in the past when the unexpected occurred? Take a moment to think about this and give thanks for unexpected gifts of the past that have shaped who you are and the path you have travelled.

Baby, Stay Calm Inside:
- Are you so focused on your own tough situation that you've allowed it to rob any joy you are feeling this season?
- Is there anyone in your life who needs something that you have to give?
- Pay it forward in simple ways. You could buy coffee for the person in front of you in line, hold a door open at the post office, or help someone carry their packages to their car. Notice how you feel after you give.

24

Disappointing Gifts

CAN WE GET real for a minute? Most of us have received gifts we don't like—maybe even gifts that deeply disappoint us. Every year, I hear from women who, after all the work of "putting on the holiday" for everyone else, are left feeling frustrated, tired, and sad because they did not feel seen or appreciated in the gifts they received.

If gifts are your love language, and you find yourself often disappointed during the holidays, read on.

We often say that the holidays are not about gifts. Yet if we're honest, we have to admit that gifts do affect our holiday experience. There are unspoken rules and cultural norms when it comes to gift giving and receiving, says Carnegie Mellon University researcher Dr. Jeff Galak. Unspoken expectations often direct givers *not* to ask what the recipient desires (so as not to ruin the surprise). Those same expectations instruct receivers not to ask for something specific and also never to say that the gift was unwanted or undesirable (so the giver never truly learns).

This cultural norm—of not talking about gifts and of loading them with unspoken expectations—is not healthy. I can recall many holidays when Ed asked me what I wanted. "Oh, nothing, really!" I'd say brightly. Yet "nothing" was code for "Don't even think about doing nothing. And do you really have to ask me by now?" The poor guy. No wonder so many people are disappointed during the holidays!

I decided to ask some people about the worst gift they ever received. The responses from my Instagram followers were both hilarious (although probably not in the moment) and revealing:

"Scarves and sweater vests . . . I live in Florida."
"An oversized T-shirt with a very large airbrushed Bambi-like deer."
"A full-body adult swaddle sleep cocoon."
"A fabric lasagna pan cover . . . I've never made lasagna."
"A pimple popper as seen on *Shark Tank*."
"Full set of copper pans . . . postpartum."

But this one takes the cake: "My then-boyfriend told me he left me a surprise in my car. I ran to the car imagining, 'Flowers, chocolate covered strawberries?' Yet in my front seat was none other than a Thigh Master. . . . I was 90 lbs., soaking wet!" (Not a surprise that this boyfriend never graduated to husband.)

As I read the responses, I couldn't help but wonder how these gifts inspired the giver to think of the recipient. I mean, how does an airbrushed deer shirt remind you of your loved one? And even if it does, what in God's earth would make you think it would be a great gift? The receiver is often wondering these questions as well: Does this gift reflect that you know me? Does the effort you put into selecting it show that you care? That's quite a weighty responsibility for a graphic tee.

My Instagram followers also shared with me some of the *best* gifts they received. Sure enough, they were not the most costly or expensive. These memorable items were thoughtful gifts that reflected something about the person receiving it. Some of these included

"a gratitude journal from a friend because I helped her succeed at work."

"a several month supply of dry shampoo when I was a brand-new mom."

"a new backing to my favorite college blanket that was frayed."

Many of the people I polled added that experience gifts—such as cooking classes, a weekend away, or vacations where memories were made—proved to be the best gifts of all.

When you receive a disappointing gift, it can be helpful to ask yourself these questions: Does this person show love and appreciate me in other ways? What are the strengths of our relationship? Have *I* ever given a gift that was not appreciated or chosen one in a rush that wasn't so thoughtful?

We often lose sight of the bigger picture when we receive a disappointing gift, and these questions can bring that back into focus. Thinking about when we may have disappointed someone else may also enable us to offer grace in this specific situation. Recognize that if you are a thoughtful giver, gifts may be more important to you than they are to most people. But remember, gift giving is simply not everyone's forte.

If you are a thoughtful giver, gifts may be more important to you than they are to most people. But remember, gift giving is simply not everyone's forte.

Dr. Galak offers some ideas for reducing the disappointments around gift giving. He revealed on the *Hidden Brain* podcast that he and his wife share a Google spreadsheet. Throughout the year, they each add items to the list that they would love to receive as a gift that they wouldn't buy for themselves. Each will then choose from the list for each occasion that warrants a gift. In this way, they receive something they actually want, but there still is an element of surprise. Apps like Giftful utilize a similar concept and allow you to include links and photos of the items. This app has been lifesaving and time-saving for buying gifts that my teens truly want and appreciate!

Personally, I always buy myself a few gifts at Christmas. They are usually small, like a new eye shadow palette or fun earrings. But it gives me something to look forward to, and I am guaranteed to receive something I like. That is part of my holiday self-care.

Hopefully you won't find yourself disappointed this holiday. But if you do, think about what you have read in these pages. It is worth some time and consideration to think about how to make the experience a little less stressful and more joyful for all.

Baby, Stay Calm Inside:
- Take a moment to consider what the true gifts are in your life right now. What would change your life irreversibly if you lost it tomorrow?
- Consider whether you are appreciating and celebrating those gifts right now. If you find yourself disappointed by the smaller things, take a moment to sit with that thought.

25

A Tale of Two Christmases

"WELL, KIDS, HERE'S one good thing: you are going to have two Christmases!"

That was the pitch my good friend and comedian Tim Washer used with his kids as they talked about holidays amid the life-altering transition of divorce. Tim is one of the few people I know who can talk about the pain and heartbreak a family endures through divorce and still make you laugh out loud. I knew he would have wisdom to share on how to navigate the complications of holidays amid divorce or how to support someone you love going through it.

If you are parenting through divorce, it is challenging to manage your own intense feelings of loss while supporting the big feelings your kids may have, too. On top of that, creating a memorable and joyful holiday in the middle of those feelings is quite a feat. Divorce also poses the additional stressor of coming to agreements with the other parent on dates, times, places, experiences and sometimes even gifts. This can create conflict and add serious tension on top of an already stressful situation.

Throughout my career as a therapist, I have gained the utmost respect for parents in these situations during the holidays. Rarely have I seen co-parents always agreeable and on the same page this time of year. If this is you and you are managing *all* of this, please believe me: you are amazing.

For that reason, let's take care of you first.

Think about what you need. Tim recalls that he knew his first Christmas Day without his kids would be devastating, so he scheduled his flight back home to Texas on Christmas morning. He knew he needed to be with his family and his friends from church—those who shared his faith and could support him on that day. Loneliness can be debilitating during the holidays, and Tim recommends reaching out to friends. He also found support in a local running community. "Runners are optimistic and healthy," he told me. "They invest in their well-being." He knew he needed to be around such people.

Some theorists believe that you become the average of the five people you spend the most time with. Research in neural synchronization appears to agree, as our brains synchronize with the people around us and those with whom we share close relationships. How true is this? Well, a few years after meeting these friends, Tim, who was never a runner, ran a marathon. "Choose your friends carefully," he advises, "and be careful not to make bad dating decisions right now. Loneliness can make you lower your standards."

Name your feelings. Tim shared that he would do this when the loneliness would hit him out of nowhere. "I could be watching *Good Luck Charlie*, and I would really miss my kids, and I would mourn the loss of the holiday spirit." Identifying the emotion helped him.

Research supports the validity of the "name it to tame it" response, as naming helps the brain to categorize and sort the emotion and therefore work through it. Tim also says not to be surprised when emotions come out at your kids. They will. "If I snapped at them, I would always apologize. You have to own it. I would say, 'I shouldn't be taking this out on you. What I need to do is go for a run. Would you forgive me, and when I come back, can we cook dinner together?'"

Anticipate your triggers. Tim prepared for the moments that he knew would be hard. "Ornaments from places that triggered sadness: I got rid of them. Holiday songs that brought back memories: I replaced them with a new playlist. And Christmas cards: I just didn't do them."

As I have said to many clients over the years, right now, it's about what feels healing to you. You want to do the cards? Do them. You don't? Then don't! There is no right or wrong, but there is a right for *you*. Tim also stresses that it's important to leave the "Why me?" questions for another time. "They take you down this death-spiral pity party, leaving you stuck. Instead, I would take a walk and spend time in nature. It would get me unstuck."

Tim also suggests looking for opportunities to be social. He says, "There is a tendency to withdraw. Before you get an invite to that holiday party, think of who you could go with. Find people who will say, 'I'll meet you there,' or 'I'll pick you up, and we can go together.' It's okay to say, 'I don't want to be around people right now.' But I knew it would be better for me to go with an exit strategy than to not go at all."

Tim has two teenage kids now. His youngest was only seven years old when the divorce happened, and going back and forth between homes was tough. Even though you want this time to be joyful for the kids, it's so important that you make sure to normalize big feelings. Some helpful things to tell children include the following: "It's okay to feel sad and mad that this happened"; "I'm sorry that you feel hurt right now, and you have every right to feel that way"; "I understand that you don't want to go to the concert tonight; it must be hard to not have both of your parents there." At the same time, reassure them that you will be there to comfort them and keep them safe. Say something like, "This is new for me, too, and we are going to figure it out together."

Tim and his kids found joy in creating new traditions. For kids, the loss of control is frightening, and so offering them options where they *do* have control can be helpful. Tim shares that he asked his kids these questions: "What did you like that we did for the holidays before, and what didn't you like? Is there anything you think would be fun for us to do together?" Sometimes, Tim says, kids have a hard time imagining new traditions, "so you have to offer them options—like travelling, if you can, and trying something new."

Tim and his kids created a new tradition in the wake of the divorce. They go into New York City the night before Thanksgiving to watch the inflating of the balloons for the Macy's parade. They cut down a tree each year at a Christmas tree farm. "I made a whole big deal about it," Tim says. "Hot chocolate, a decorating party . . . I leaned into *their* joy. We even made a gingerbread house for the first time!" Even during the hardest season of his life, Tim knew there was joy to be had, and he found it.

For many parents, interacting with the other parent can be challenging. Tim suggests that lowering expectations of what you expect them to do can be helpful. "Then it becomes less frustrating when they resist, and it doesn't create chaos for your life." Tim also made an intentional effort to speak kindly about the kids' mother by finding positive qualities to share. "Your mother is so organized, and I am not. Your mother and I love you both so very much. Hey—let's text a picture of you two to your mom." He admits this can be hard at times, but it can be helpful for the child's healing process. At the end of the day, you can't control what the other parent chooses to do. If they want to make the holiday difficult—as life coach Mel Robbins advises—"Let them." Then redirect your focus to what you *can* control such as creating a holiday experience that you want to share with your kids.

Tim tells me about one holiday early in the aftermath of the divorce. His own mother was also living with dementia and would ask the same questions over and over again. "This is soul-crushing stuff," he says: "divorce and dementia."

Yet this particular visit to his mother has become one of his family's favorite holiday memories. His mother really wanted to take his kids to Toys "R" Us to pick out Christmas gifts and then out to lunch. The kids had a blast at the toy store, picking out what they wanted. Tim, the children, and his mother had a nice lunch afterward. "As we ended, my mom turned to the kids and said, 'I would love to take you both to Toys "R" Us!' The kids looked at me, surprised, but said nothing."

"What did you say?" I ask.

Tim replies with a touch of his Texas twang. "'Come on! Let's go!' My mom just loved it (again). And the kids thought it was the greatest thing in the world."

"Don't worry," Tim tells me, "This time the gifts were just five dollars." I laugh out loud. Tim smiles.

A tale of two Christmases indeed.

Baby, Stay Calm Inside:
- Is there something that might be "right" for the holidays but not right for you at this time? Save it for another holiday when it feels like the right moment.
- What do you need this holiday to feel connected and calm?

- Do you have a friend or loved one going through a divorce? Reach out to them today. Let them know that you are thinking of them. Invite them to a gathering, make time for coffee, or schedule time to drop off a note or a small thoughtful gift. These are the times when it will mean the most.

26

Presence over Presents

WHAT DO YOU want to remember when the holiday is over? I asked myself this question as I wrote this book, and I imagine you may ask it too. Many of us want to remember things like seeing our kids' faces on Christmas morning; gathering with family and friends; doing activities like baking cookies and attending holiday concerts; collecting gifts and dropping them off for kids who need them; and, of course, laughing and dozing during late-night classic holiday movie marathons.

Then I asked myself a harder question: But what do you *actually* remember? Try asking that one yourself.

I thought back to the last holiday. Maybe it's my perimenopausal mind, which seems to have a mind of its own, but honestly, I could not remember much. The memories over the years seemed to blur together, and nothing specific came to mind. I could not recall one gift I received, although I know there were many that I appreciated. On the flip side, I also couldn't remember any holiday drama—and there is always some of that, too! Sometimes forgetting might be the gift that keeps on giving.

There are positives to documenting much of our lives on our phones (although you won't catch me saying that very often). I took a look back at my photos, and many of the things that I wanted to remember came back to me: a visit from our town Grinch and my daughter biting into the raw onion he offered her, doing a fun holiday segment for the *TODAY Show*, getting sparkly red nails done with my daughters, and dressing the entire family in Christmas Eve pj's with funny titles to reflect each person. I couldn't really remember any of it until I looked at my phone. It sure looked like we had ourselves a great holiday!

But why couldn't I remember? I have a few thoughts on this. Like many of you, I run around like crazy in December, focused on things that never make my "want to remember" list. My brain is in overdrive—although I still find some time for mindless scrolling. Even though I speak and write about *not* scrolling, social media is so addictive, especially during the holidays. Many of us long to see what everyone else is doing and how they are doing it. All of this not only affects my ability to be present, but it also affects my experience of events as they are happening. Let me explain.

I wrote extensively about screens in my first book, and how they hijack our neural pathways and prevent us from being fully *present* and connecting with those around us. Since then, even more psychologists and authors have written about the negative impact of screens. Screens are one of the reasons that we lose our ability to be present as life happens around us.

During the holidays, when many of us are tired and overwhelmed, I can guarantee our phone usage increases. Between holiday shopping and seeing how friends on social media are celebrating, we make ourselves captive audiences.

When we constantly thought switch—from one image or post to another, which apps are designed to make us do—we leave a residue of attention behind on the last thing we saw. Our full attention has not been fully transferred to the next thing. The flow of neural energy through our brain circuitry is disrupted. This creates what some neuroscientists refer to as a "milkshake brain"—one that is easily distracted with a limited attention span. Limited attention spans translate into a limited ability to recall and remember.

Please remember that I, too, struggle with putting down my phone. When I am at my busiest, my kids often say to me, "Mom, finish your sentence!" Because my thoughts are switching so fast, I often stop speaking mid-sentence. My brain has already moved on to the next thing. Does this sound like someone who is present?

I know if I want to be more present, experience my life more fully, and actually remember this time of year, one thing I can do is limit my screen usage. I think it's safe to say that most of us would benefit from less phone time.

But do you know how screens also affect our mood? At this point, we have all heard about the addictive nature of dopamine hits. Dopamine is that feel-good neurochemical responsible for new pleasure, reward, and motivation. But have you heard about the dopamine deficit that occurs to compensate for those continuous hits?

I'm sure you have seen a child who has been on an iPad for a while and how they react when it's taken away, and I'm sure you know the behavior that ensues. Yelling, anger, tears, inability to cope: if it looks like withdrawal symptoms, it's because it could be. Psychiatrist Anna Lembke explains the concept of a dopamine deficit in her bestselling book, *Dopamine Nation*. When our brains are exposed to constant dopamine hits, our dopamine levels surge. In order for the body to maintain homeostasis, or a steady state of dopamine, the brain needs to downregulate dopamine, or bring it to a lower state (deficit) than what we actually need to restore balance in the body. In this deficit state, we experience more sadness, anxiety, and depression as well as an inability to cope with stress and, in more extreme situations, suicidal ideation. I truly believe this is one of the reasons we are seeing more young people of the ages eleven to fourteen presenting with more anxiety, depression, and suicidal ideation. It's the physiological compensation for constant high levels of dopamine.

I know that a lecture on dopamine is not what you envisioned when you picked up a holiday book! But hear me out. I tell you this because, for many of you, holidays are frantic and don't feel festive. You want to feel calmer, more content, and more present, but your life contains real stressors, many of which you cannot control.

Here's the thing: screens are one of the factors you *can* control. Reducing your usage will indeed help your mood.

For years, when I treated patients with anxiety, I would always recommend a ten-day phone detox. Never once did a patient return saying, "It didn't help." Each person said they felt different after limiting screen use. I used to think it was because they weren't on Instagram, comparing their lives, which perhaps is part of it. Now I know, it was more than that. We were restoring a healthier balance of dopamine and likely getting them out of a deficit.

So, how do we cultivate more presence this holiday?

First, *let go of the little things.* The guests arrived late, you burned the cookies or didn't make them at all, you're stressed about going or not going to the party: if it doesn't make your "want to remember" list, then don't give it your valuable attention or energy. Let's direct that elsewhere.

Second, *intentionally limit your screen time.* Screen time limits only do so much; most of us override them. Put your phone away where you can't see it for certain hours of the day, such as meals, conversations, and events. Delete social media or YouTube from your phone for seventy-two hours and see how you feel. (This one action is incredibly revealing.) Smart watches are often a good alternative to carrying around that distraction device. It's the main reason I got one: to be more present. It helps. Also, leave a good book or festive magazine in the places in the house where you tend to scroll. Good old-fashioned reading is a much healthier replacement behavior—and who doesn't want to read more?

Third, intentionally *make time for healthy dopamine-stimulating activities.* What are those moments you want to

What are those moments you want to remember? What would help you to feel calmer during your day? remember? What would help you to feel calmer during your day? A brisk morning walk in nature; taking in a sunrise or sunset; making cookies with a friend; an afternoon nap if you aren't sleeping well; reading a chapter of that good book (I guarantee you could finish this one if you picked it up daily instead of checking your phone); listening to holiday music; lifting weights; spending moments in silence, prayer, or meditation: all will stimulate healthy levels of dopamine, help to regulate your mood, and bring more presence into this holiday. Pick one of these a day, even if it's for five minutes. A little in this area will go a long way.

I challenge you to try some of these suggestions and perhaps next year you won't need your phone to remember some of the joy of this holiday. Presence is the best present indeed.

Baby, Stay Calm Inside:
- Take a moment to make a "want to remember" list.
- What is the one thing you will do to replace constant scrolling this holiday?
- What could you do more or less of during your day to help you be more present? Commit to that one thing today.

27

To Holiday Card, or Not

I WOULDN'T SAY our holidays are simple. When I was a younger mom, I got caught up in starting all the traditions. Some of those I continue to this day, even though I don't always want to.

Let's take, for example, holiday cards.

Don't get me wrong: I love *receiving* other people's holiday cards with their festive family photos and personal updates. Yet, creating and sending our cards stresses me out. What started out as a simple wedding photo, printed on a Costco holiday card the first year we were married, has evolved into quite a complicated beast. We coordinate our outfits, find the right location, and hire a professional photographer: as crazy as this sounds, this is common in my area. I *do* realize not everyone does this, and I am sure it sounds a little obnoxious and *a lot* privileged. But I started something that now I continue annually, which often adds more stress than anyone needs. Try to get teens to smile for a pic when they just had a blowout argument, let alone coordinate outfits when all they want to wear is a graphic tee and sweats with holes.

Several years ago, as life got busier, I found myself asking, "Do I really want to do this?"

Every holiday, several of my friends reach out and say, "Loved your card, but I decided I'm not doing cards this year. Too stressful! Maybe next year." I appreciate those messages, and my first thought is always "good for you!" These women are able to step out of the confines of what no longer serves them and make a better decision, based on their needs in real time. I think I am somewhat jealous, too, because I often have a hard time doing this, especially during the holidays. I often set an expectation for myself about something I should do, and then each time I do it, it gets harder and harder to hop off that relentless hamster wheel.

Can we talk about "should" statements again? These subtle but powerful thoughts, which we may not even be aware of, strongly influence our decisions and behaviors. Comparison often tends to be the catalyst for these thoughts. But during the holidays, well-established traditions play into them as well. One thing is for sure—a *should* is always connected to an expectation:

> *I'm exhausted but I should go to that holiday party because everyone will be there. I should put up the tree this year, even though I just can't seem to motivate myself since my mom passed away. Our elf should be as creative and naughty as their elf.*

I should bake twelve dozen cookies this year, but that will mean no sleep for a few nights. I should have a partner by now, but I guess I'll spend another holiday alone.

I said it once, and I will say it again: stop "shoulding" on yourself.

At their best, "should" statements can give us the push we need to do the thing we don't feel like doing; the outcome can be enjoyable. When *shoulds* align with what we value, they can be motivational. Yet, I find that clients who constantly "should" themselves to do things out of guilt and obligation end up feeling resentful and drained. Certainly not how we want to feel during the holidays.

At their worst, "should" statements reflect expectations placed on us by others or our environment and make us feel frustrated and discontented with our own life situation. They can prevent us from seeing what is good and beneficial and force us to myopically focus on an unmet expectation.

Like most of life these days, the holidays go by in a blink. Don't we want to spend that time in meaningful and memorable ways?

I now recognize that if a "should" statement is a part of my decision to do something, I need to pause and evaluate if it's truly worth it. What will this decision cost me or those around me? Whose expectation is it? How will I feel after?

What would I rather be doing? What would be the worst-case scenario if I didn't do it? How would it benefit me or those around me to do it differently or not do it? The cost of a decision can be time, finances, energy, mental health, or even a relationship if it creates stress between people. It's so important, especially during this unusually busy season, to consider the cost and ask the following question: is it worth it?

With "should" statements come pressure. I often encourage my clients to replace the *should* with *want* or *would like to*. As we saw in an earlier chapter, that simple word change releases some of the pressure but preserves our good intentions. Sometimes that switch, in and of itself, helps us to find a much-needed perspective shift and make a better choice. Instead of "I should send two hundred cards out this year," I might say, "I would like to send out cards." A reframe can alleviate some of the pressure and allow for more grace.

Grace is something we all need during the holidays. Most of us have a lot of it for others and very little for ourselves. Self-compassion is the pathway to grace. When we can have the same empathy for ourselves as we would for a friend in the same situation, we can find our voice of self-compassion. Think about what you would say to a friend asking for your advice. So I may say to myself now, "I want to send out cards this year, but

> **Grace is something we all need during the holidays. Most of us have a lot of it for others and very little for ourselves.**

it's been such a stressful season, and I would rather spend that time connecting with my family and doing more restful things. Maybe next year."

Truth be told, I still send out the cards. I save them each year, and I enjoy looking back and remembering our family captured in that moment in time. And it just might be the only photo I actually print out of the 8,759 I take annually.

But I did have a year where I found an ounce of grace for myself. That year, instead of hiring a photographer and stressing about a location or outfits, I yelled upstairs to the kids, "Find your holiday pj's from a Christmas or two ago and meet us downstairs in ten minutes!"

The Christmas tree was far from decorated, but we did have a festive wreath lit above the fireplace. The kids, comfy and cozy, stood in front of it while I snapped a quick photo with my phone. When a holiday photo takes less than five minutes in your pj's and you don't even need to leave your house—well, all *is* calm.

Upload, order, print, and mail: that was it. Good enough is both good and enough. To this day, that card will always be one of my favorites—for more reasons than one.

Baby, Stay Calm Inside:
- Is there anything you do during the holidays that makes you feel drained or resentful? Are you aware of any "should" statements at work here?

- What would the holiday be like if you didn't do it or did it differently for this one year? What would be the benefit to you and those around you?
- If it would make your holiday a little more festive and less frantic or give you a little more peace this year, I encourage you to make that change. Try it this year and see what happens!

28

If You Believe

IT IS MY honor to share with you one of my favorite Christmas stories. This is a true story about the possibility of miracles. My husband's Uncle Charlie Rivera read this story to our family a few weeks before Christmas. When Uncle Charlie shared his story, he reflected upon a few questions, which I have thought about and put into my own words at the end of the chapter. I share them with you to think about in this season of miracles.

Here's Uncle Charlie's story:

As a young boy I grew up in New Jersey. At that time, we were a family of six: my parents, three brothers, and me. Although we weren't quite poor or destitute, we were far from being considered lower middle class.

It was Christmas Eve in 1961. Just twelve days before my sixth birthday. I vividly recall huddling around our old black-and-white television, watching *The Ed Sullivan Show*. We four brothers were all happy, excited, and giddy anticipating Santa's arrival.

Yet unlike years past, our parents did not seem joyful. In fact, they appeared quite the opposite. My dad sat in his chair silent and sullen, while my mom sat by herself, subdued. She held a rosary in her hand and quietly prayed.

Unexpectedly, my mom stood up, walked to the television, and turned it off. In a voice full of genuine sorrow, she said to us, "This year Santa Claus will not be visiting our home."

We four brothers looked at our mom, confused, not quite understanding what she meant. She repeated herself, her voice cracking: "This Christmas, Santa Claus will not be coming here. There is no money for toys or presents."

Almost in unison, we blurted out, "But Mom, what does money have to do with it?" One brother said, "Everybody knows that Santa and the elves make the toys!" And another: "And we've been good all year long!"

With that, my dad, his voice much louder and sterner than my mother's, declared, "There is no such thing as Santa!" He was visibly troubled but continued: "Mom and I are Santa. And this year we cannot afford to buy any of you presents or toys."

My brothers and I were shocked by what we heard. No Santa? No toys? No Christmas? This couldn't be. Witnessing the distress of our parents was also difficult. My mom returned to her chair to cry and pray some more, and my dad paced back and forth.

We brothers all just sat there on the floor silently, saddened and utterly confused by what just occurred. The clock slowly ticked away the minutes toward the midnight hour.

What happened next can only be understood if you believe in miracles.

A little after 10 p.m., we heard a knock on the door. My dad, totally bewildered as to who could possibly be visiting us at this hour, opened the door. Seeing who was there, he turned around and looked at my mom. His face was pale, as if he had just seen a ghost. My mom approached the door, peered out, and was equally shocked at our unexpected guest.

My brothers and I heard the ringing of bells and a deep, raspy, and completely recognizable voice saying, "Ho, ho, ho! Merry Christmas!"

We rushed to the door, ecstatic. Santa had come to our home after all. The four of us started jumping and screaming with delight.

"We *told* you that Santa was real!" we kept saying to our parents. "We told you!"

Santa walked in, knew us all by name, and proceeded to give each of us our very own Christmas gift. He stayed only for a few minutes. But to this day, I can clearly see my mother looking at Santa, tears running down her face, and her saying to him in a soft, quivering voice, "I believe. I believe."

With God as my witness, I can honestly say this to all of you: that single act of love more than fifty-five years ago changed my life forever. I'm sure my brothers would all say the same. For you see, that kind soul, whoever he was—who probably thought he'd brought joy to a few little kids for a single day—would never know how much that evening meant. He probably doesn't know that every holiday season that has gone by since then, at least one of us shares the true and miraculous story of when Santa Claus came to town.

And so, on that day I learned that these three remain: faith, hope, and love. And the greatest of these is love (1 Corinthians 13:13).

> ***Soul-Full Season from Uncle Charlie:*** Is my *faith* in God as strong as a mother's praying with all her might for God to intercede at the most difficult of times? Is my *hope* and anticipation for the birth of Christ and God's presence in my life as awakened and as joyful as it was when I was a young boy looking forward to the arrival of Santa? Is my *love* for my neighbors as real, personal, and unconditional as the love a stranger showed to a struggling family so many years ago? And finally, when it comes to faith and miracles, can I firmly say, "I believe. I believe"?

> ***Baby, Stay Calm Inside:***
> - We all have the capacity to be a part of a miracle. Can you think of anything you can do to participate in someone else's miracle? Start with the needs around you.
> - Is there anything this holiday that can awaken that childlike joy within you? Connect with that part of you; make time for whatever it is that can make you feel that way even for a few moments.

29

Wonder

WHEN WAS THE last time you wondered about anything? When did you last sit with a question and consider the vast possibilities that could be answers? I mean, when was the last time you actually did that?

My oldest daughter Natalia wonders all the time. I didn't fully appreciate this until our recent trip to the Grand Canyon. As we stood there on the edge, in awe of the breathtaking landscape, she asked quietly, "I wonder how old that steam engine is?" With a furrowed brow, she gazed at the vintage steam-powered train in the distance, which stood out against the canyon's terracotta-colored cliffs and sweeping vistas.

I hadn't even noticed the train.

Her question hung in the stillness. The train seemed out of place like a relic from another time, and yet it sparked her imagination and curiosity. I could see a deeper level of thinking occurring. She began to speak of the stories she had learned in her AP history class, such as the Homestead Act of 1862 and how steam engines enabled the expansion into the area, leading to its settlement. In that moment, it became clear to me how deeply she engages with the world around her. Although her lengthy explanation and curiosity about the train's age was lost on me, she did not do what I would have done from the get-go.

She never pulled out her phone.

That's what we do now, isn't it? We answer our questions as soon as we have them. Most of the answers can be found at our fingertips. **We no longer wonder and ponder and imagine, engaging our own curiosity and entertaining possibility.** In the instant gratification that we seek, we have lost something invaluable and once inextricable from our human experience: wonder.

During childhood, wonder is second nature. We especially see it in children this time of year. Eyes wide with excitement as they anticipate the arrival of Santa, in awe of how he gets the job done all over the world and on time. All it takes are twinkling lights, sugar-sparkled cookies, or a wrapped gift to awaken joy and magic in a child. Yet, as adults, we find wonder much harder to come by. This is especially true during the holidays with our lists and schedules and late nights. Sometimes I wonder, Can we get it back?

My friend Carlos Whittaker, author of *Reconnected*, has something to say about wonder. *Reconnected* details his seven-week experiment of living screen-free. During that time, Carlos lived in a monastery and on an Amish farm. For nearly two months, Carlos was forced to wait—and wonder—when he had a question or a thought. "Wondering *leads* to wonder," he tells me. "We lose our sense of wonder when we are no longer wondering."

Carlos is a well-known influencer and podcaster. If anyone understands the impact of being on phones, it's him. He also now understands what life feels like without them.

During those seven weeks, left alone with his thoughts uninterrupted by notifications and unable to satisfy sudden impulses to scroll, he did a lot of thinking. Not only did he discover that wondering leads to wonder, but he also found that *waiting* also leads to wonder.

Brain scans before and after the experiment revealed that Carlos's brain changed for the better after eliminating technology. He confirms that his life changed for the better too. No longer does he use a phone as an alarm clock; he relies on an actual clock to get him out of bed. "Phones are out of the room," he says. "That automatically knocked off two hours of screen time between the morning and evening." Multitasking is out, and single tasking is in. Carlos has even gotten into the habit of reading a physical newspaper in the mornings rather than consuming reels on social media.

Carlos finds that without the constant pull of screens, life feels different. Simple experiences, like savoring his morning coffee or noticing dew drops on his boots, bring wonder. He tells me that even conversations with other people feel different; he feels a deeper sense of presence and therefore connection with people.

I don't know about you, but I want more of a life like this . . . *desperately*. For those of you old enough to know life before constant technology: do you feel the nostalgia that I do? I think of my college days when we had to call each other on our dorm room landlines to make plans to have coffee. I think of how often we spent time together in person, in connected conversations. What better time of year to bring some of this back?

"So, how might this holiday look different than those of the past?" I ask Carlos. With his newfound sense wonder, what about the holidays has changed?

"If you look around at holiday parties, everyone pulls phones out as soon as you ask a question," he says. "Let's not do that. Let's ask a question, sit with it, and watch the conversations happen. We miss so much by not wondering. Maybe we will have some 'aha' moments. The longer you wonder, the bigger the 'aha' moment." And who doesn't want more "aha" moments?

When I think of times that I have truly had such a moment, I realize that they happened while I was sitting with a thought or observing events unfolding. Rarely did an "aha" moment come while I was being fed information constantly.

Such moments of instant gratification and knowledge are quickly forgotten.

Carlos's book will make me think about this holiday differently. I want to discover what wonder looks like as an adult. I want to experience connected presence when I am with those I love, uninterrupted, taking in what I see and feel, observing and savoring these beautiful yet fleeting moments.

We take one step closer to wonder when we deny the impulse to immediately satisfy and gratify the need to know. When we resist the desire to disconnect from real life and to numb our tired minds—such as deciding *not* to escape boredom by pulling out a phone while waiting in line—we begin to practice curiosity and engage our imaginations like we did when we were kids. We settle into actual living and get comfortable with our thoughts. We allow for a deeper awareness of ourselves and the world around us. That sounds like the beginning of wonder.

We take one step closer to wonder when we deny the impulse to immediately satisfy and gratify the need to know.

I asked Natalia why she didn't pull out her phone that day to answer her own question, like so many of us would do. It was strange to me that she didn't.

"Maybe it's laziness," she replied. "But I think I like to wonder."

Soul-Full Season: Wonder can often help in times of uncertainty. We might wonder how God will show up in a situation that is full of unknowns or wonder how God will resolve an issue you may be facing today. Wonder can be a practice of faith. Take a few moments to wonder and imagine the possibilities that would bring hope and even joy.

Baby, Stay Calm Inside:
- Where do you find that you are choosing a screen over engaging in real life? Can you take a small step to reduce those moments? Maybe it means phones out of the bedroom or away from the dinner table. Pick one and try it this holiday.
- Most of us will spend time waiting in lines this holiday or maybe sitting in a waiting room. What if you could see these as opportunities for wonder? Look around you and see how long you can go without glancing at a phone. Observe those around you and see where your mind leads you.

30

Miracles in the Mess

"WHAT A MESS," I mumble under my breath, to no one in particular. It's December, and I'm surveying the state of my house. (But let's be real: I say this year-round.)

I walk into the family room, which my kids had picked up just a few days ago. It's decked out for Christmas with our winter white-and-gold sparkling fir tree in the corner. Yet, right in the middle of the room, there is a rogue soccer ball, blankets tossed haphazardly on the couches from last night's movie, a trail of stale popcorn leading to a half-empty mug of cold cocoa, and a few paperback novels with fluorescent Post-it tabs sticking out, reminders of someone's high school lit class. I sigh, taking in the scene. Just another day in the Feliciano household.

Our home has a rhythm: every three days it vacillates from calm, relatively organized, and peaceful to cluttered, chaotic, and disarrayed. I've come to realize that my house often mirrors the state of my life . . . especially when I am deep in the process of writing a book.

As a therapist, I'm no stranger to mess. I know this time of year feels particularly messy for many of us—and that the mess is far more complex than a disorganized family room. There is marriage mess, financial mess, parenting mess, cancer mess, loneliness mess. Maybe it's *you* who feels like a mess, or maybe you are trying to support a loved one in the midst of their mess. Either way, the mess does not pause for the holidays, and it often makes them harder to bear.

It wasn't supposed to look like this, right? By now, things should be different. By now, you should have it all together. But here you are, looking around your life thinking, "What a mess."

As I stand there in our family room, debating whether to start cleaning or just walk away and pretend I didn't see it, something catches my eye. It's our seventeen-year-old Fisher-Price Little People nativity set, which we bought for my oldest daughter's first Christmas. Even now, younger kids who visit our home find it magical—and I sometimes catch my own big ones still enjoying it. The cherub-like figurines stand happily under the straw roof of the manger, with their bright eyes and colorful robes. Each one, from the kings to the camels, shows a dimpled smile. At the center lies a calm, clean baby Jesus, looking like he just woke up from a perfect eight-hour nap.

But the reality of that first Christmas was far from serene. Whether you believe in the story as the birth of the long-awaited savior or just think of it as a mystical holiday tale, it's worth remembering that this scene was messy, too. It was filled with disappointment, fear, unmet expectations, grief, and crisis—not what we typically imagine as the backdrop for a miracle.

Let's consider the circumstances.

Historians tell us that Jesus's mother, Mary, was likely between thirteen and sixteen years old. In her time, it wasn't unusual to become a mother at this young age. But I can't help but marvel at how young she was to carry the weight of what was to come. I imagine that, like any young girl, she had dreams—perhaps of a joyful wedding surrounded by family and friends, a day of celebration in her small village. This would have been typical in her culture and was often the highlight of a young woman's life.

But all those dreams were turned upside down when Joseph, her fiancé, learned she was pregnant. An unwed pregnancy wasn't just a scandal; it was a crime, punishable by death, usually stoning. Joseph, heartbroken and confused, had planned to divorce her quietly, which, though merciful, would have left Mary alone, likely never to marry again, and forced to live as a single mother in a society that had no place for her. But after his encounter with an angel, he made a different decision. Instead of walking away, he chose to stay, quietly continuing their relationship without the wedding fanfare or the support of their community.

As if this stressful start were not enough, Mary and Joseph then traveled ninety miles to complete a census, prior to the birth of Jesus. Women, let's pause for a moment: this young teen was nine months pregnant, riding on a donkey, for a journey that could have taken a week. Can you even begin to imagine? God and I would have had some serious discussions that would have started with "Is this a joke? Seriously, for real?"

And it gets worse. As the story goes, there was no place for her to give birth, so they ended up in a stable. I'm going to guess this was not what Mary detailed in her birthing plan. I think about her lying there in incredible pain, surrounded by the smell and filth of animals. There were no women around to help—no mother, no aunts, no sisters who would have been her village to support her emotionally and physically. Instead, she had Joseph, a man who, by their customs, wouldn't have even been in the room during childbirth. And let's be real: she probably barely knew him. This man, who had likely never even seen her undressed, was now the one to deliver her baby? Nothing about this was normal. Yet this is exactly how Jesus came into the world. Messy, painful, completely unexpected.

But look at Mary's response at the end of the story. Despite the fear, the uncertainty, the unmet expectations, and the pain, she experienced nothing short of a miracle. Luke, the physician and disciple, writes in the scriptures that "Mary treasured up all these things, pondering them in her heart" (Luke 2:19 ESV).

What exactly was she treasuring? Was it the angel chorus that broke through the quiet of that starry night, filling the sky with heavenly song? Or the unexpected arrival of the magi, bringing lavish gifts fit for a king and kneeling before this humble family? Maybe it was simply the joy of holding her baby in her arms, this long-awaited child, knowing he would change the world someday and that she was his mama. Whatever it was, in the midst of the mess, Mary found something beautiful. She held it close and thought about it often, perhaps remembering that even in the hardest moments, God shows up and miracles happen.

At this time of year, can we do the same? Are we open to the possibility that in the middle of our messes, there are miracles to be found?

A wise psychologist once told me that I needed to accept things not for what they should be but for how they are—and look for the positive within them. So I take a deep breath, and then I take another glance around my cluttered family room. Slowly, my own little miracles come into view. I feel grateful to have four healthy kids still living under my roof who like to spend holiday evenings curled up on our comfy couches, watching Christmas movies together. Three of them love soccer, so they've always got a ball at their feet, practicing even when no one is watching. My daughter, who is ever the hard worker, sneaks in some reading during family movie nights, highlighter in hand.

Suddenly, I realize these are the blessings right in front of me . . . and they are fleeting. One day, this room will be spotless, ordered, and organized . . . and I will likely not have these particular blessings in my home any longer.

It may be harder to see the miracle in your situation, which may be far from simple. Perhaps it's the way people have shown up for you, or the moments of rest you are now forced to take. Maybe it's realizing how much someone meant to you and the gratitude you feel for having had them in your life, if only for a short time. What I do know is this: if you are open to seeing even the smallest of miracles, you will likely find one.

> **If you are open to seeing even the smallest of miracles, you will likely find one.**

The first Christmas was complicated, unexpected, and messy. It was never meant to be perfect or easy. Maybe that's the reminder we need: that it doesn't have to be. Even in the mess, there is something worth treasuring. We can still find what is most important, even beautiful; hold it close; and think of it often—perhaps for years to come.

Soul-Full Season: Ask to see the everyday miracles in your day. Write down your thoughts over the next few days on what you begin to see.

Baby, Stay Calm Inside:
- Where is life messy for you these days?
- What is still good about your life that maybe you have lost sight of in the midst of the mess? Is there a miracle that you are missing?

31

New Year, Same Me

SEVERAL YEARS AGO, I stopped making New Year's resolutions. I had started doing TV segments about mental health and relationships, and in my research for one of those interviews, I found out that only 9 percent of Americans who make New Year's resolutions actually keep them. Twenty-three percent quit by the end of the first week. Forty-three percent quit by the end of January (I was likely in this group).

I also found myself making the same resolutions year after year: lose weight, work out more, spend less time on my phone, get organized. Essentially, I would begin each year excessively focused on my flaws. So no matter how motivated I felt on day one—you know, "New Year, New You!"—I set myself up for failure. Remind me of the definition of insanity? Clearly, I was doing the same things over and over again expecting a different result yet ending at the same outcome: just start over again each January.

Before I gave up resolutions entirely, however, I got a little wiser. What if I thought in terms of *intentions* rather than resolutions? Intentions seem kinder and gentler in my mind than resolutions do—less of a "should" and more of a self-compassionate reminder. I like that intentions make room for life's unpredictability. Intentions give me space to take care of what matters most in the moment, without feeling like I am failing. Intentions give grace. I'm convinced that, with all the demands and expectations placed upon us—whether you are a stay-at-home parent or a corporate executive—we all could use a little more grace.

Yet even intentions can become simply resolutions in disguise. I can still use them to subtly remind myself that I am not enough. In 2023, I came across an article in the *New York Times*, written by Melissa Kirsch, titled "Resolving Resolutions." She writes about how resolutions can become an imaginary cudgel, "a method to get ourselves back in line, a means of eradicating parts of ourselves that we don't like."

What she says next resonates with me deeply. Resolutions tend to suggest that we are not good enough the way we are right now. "My resolutions are typically of this variety. Self-criticism designed as self-improvement," she writes. "If your resolutions seem architected by someone who doesn't like you, there's still time to reconsider it."

Hmm. That gave me something to think about.

Like many of my patients, when I start a new habit, it's full speed ahead . . . at an unsustainable pace for life with four kids and a demanding career. Research on habit formation emphasizes the collective and transformative power of small, incremental changes sustained over time. It's worth noting that anything worth doing is worth doing even a little bit.

So I accepted this truth and changed my focus. I gave up the annual tradition altogether. Once I turned forty, I stopped focusing on what I wanted to do, and instead, I began to consider *who I wanted to be*.

At the heart of habit change is identity, and when we begin to consider who we want to become, the habits follow naturally. So who do I want to be? This is the question I now sit with at this time of year. What has this last year taught me about myself? How have I gotten closer to the version of myself that is ever evolving?

> **What has this last year taught me about myself? How have I gotten closer to the version of myself that is ever evolving?**

I no longer think about losing weight, which generally implies a timeline, comparisons, and considerable pressure. Instead, I focus on becoming the healthiest version of myself. Instead of scolding myself to spend less time on my phone, I think about becoming a fully present, connected wife, mom, and friend.

One New Year's tradition I *have* embraced is choosing a word for the year. I like the idea of a word compass—a reminder of how I want to live, one that brings perspective to my experiences and directs my thoughts and actions. I don't randomly pick a word; I pray for one.

For the last fifteen years, I start my year with forty days of prayer, stillness, meditation, and some sort of fast. Fasting is a spiritual practice in my faith. We believe that by some cosmic principle, fasting and sacrifice tells God, "Hey, I'm serious." It has worked for me and many of the women who have embarked on this annual journey with me. During this time, I read scripture daily and pray for direction, for my family, for opportunities, and for specific requests that I or others may have. I also pray for my word.

This past year, the word that I felt strongly connected to was *aligned*. This word made perfect sense as I entered my late forties. I wanted my words, my actions, and my life to be aligned with my priorities, my values, and my faith. *Aligned* served as a reminder to keep it all in check.

Obviously, as a therapist, I am all about changing habits and setting goals. But this year, can we do it with a little more grace? Instead of only focusing on what needs to change, let's recognize how in some ways we're already becoming the person we want to be. What's working already? What gets in the way of you fully being that person? What is one thing you can add to move closer to that vision? If you still want to make a resolution, how about adding "whenever possible" at the end? Automatic grace.

> **What's working already? What gets in the way of you fully being that person? What is one thing you can add to move closer to that vision?**

In his best-selling book *Atomic Habits*, James Clear shares a simple yet powerful idea that has stayed with me: in a world where everyone is striving to be the most interesting person in the room, instead try to be the most interested person in the room. Because if we are the most interested person in the room, we are the things most of us desire to become these days: present, curious, connected, empathic, and humble. Clear goes on to write about how interested people are also the most successful by virtue of the opportunities that open up to those who live this way.

So if you are still looking for a resolution, maybe this is the one: be interested.

Baby, Stay Calm Inside:
- Think about the year that is almost past. What have you learned about yourself? How have you gotten closer to the version of yourself that is ever evolving?
- If you were to choose a word for the year ahead, what might it be? You may want to mull over this question for a bit, or journal or pray about it. What word do you feel drawn to as you think about who you want to be in the coming year?

Well, you made it to the end of this book! This is where we part ways. Thank you for going on this journey with me. Even if you didn't read it all, my hope is that you read what you needed at the time you needed it most. I hope you can carry a little bit of the beauty, the perspective, and the calm(*ish*) sense that you found in this season into the rest of the year. Let this book be a reminder that you did it and can do it again.

Wishing you a year of grace, growth, and peace—whenever possible.

Ten Ideas to Keep the Holidays Simple and Memorable

- **Build Your Own Hot Chocolate Bar:** Set up a cozy station with different flavors of cocoa, whipped cream, marshmallows, peppermint sticks, and fun toppings like crushed candy canes, chocolate shavings, sprinkles, and cinnamon. Add festive mugs and let everyone create their own delicious winter treat.
- **Have Marathon Movie Nights in Holiday Pajamas:** Snuggle up in the coziest holiday pj's, grab some blankets, and watch your favorite holiday movies. Let each family member pick a movie, from classic favorites to new releases, making it a night full of laughter, nostalgia, and fun!
- **Enjoy an Evening Drive Through a Festively Lit Neighborhood:** Pack some blankets and hot drinks, put on a holiday playlist, and take a slow drive through neighborhoods twinkling with festive lights. Enjoy the magic of the season as you marvel at the creative displays, from elegant white lights to houses covered in colorful decor.
- **Make a Gingerbread House Decorating Extravaganza:** Get creative with gingerbread houses! For

little ones, assemble the houses beforehand to avoid frustration, then let the decorating begin with icing, gumdrops, candy canes, and sprinkles galore.

- **Relax with a Glass or a Mug by a Roaring Fire:** After the kids are tucked in, unwind by the fire with a glass of wine, your favorite festive drink, or a hot cup of tea. Let the warmth of the flames and the flicker of the lights melt away the day's stress while you enjoy some much-needed peace and quiet.
- **Sip Morning Coffee with a Glow:** Start your day in a magical way by sipping your coffee or tea in front of the soft glow of the Christmas tree, a beautifully lit menorah, or the wintry comfort of a pine-scented candle. Take a quiet moment to reflect and breathe in the holiday spirit.
- **Create a Personalized Ornament:** Choose a favorite photo that reminds you of a special moment from this year and craft a homemade ornament. Whether it's a family vacation, a milestone, or a memory you want to cherish, this DIY tradition will help you carry these moments into the new year.
- **Try Coquito (If you know, you know.):** For a taste of the holidays in Puerto Rico, whip up a batch of coquito, the creamy coconut rum drink that's a holiday favorite. (The Goya recipe is our fav!) Rich, indulgent, and full of island flavors, this festive drink will bring some tropical cheer to your celebration.

- **Bake Cookies and Spread Holiday Cheer:** Spend an afternoon baking a variety of holiday cookies, from sugar cookies to spiced gingerbread, and package them in festive tins. Deliver the goodies to a neighbor or someone in need of some extra cheer. If you've got the energy for it, make it a tradition to try a new recipe every year!
- **Give Back as a Family:** Embrace the true spirit of the season by serving as a family. Sponsor a family in need, collect canned goods for a local food bank, or make homemade cards for nursing home residents or children in hospitals. It's a wonderful way to spread joy and teach your family the value of generosity.

ACKNOWLEDGMENTS

BELIEVE ME WHEN I say this book is a miracle. In addition to God making things possible when you think it's absolutely impossible, there are many people who made this happen both knowingly and unknowingly.

First of all, thank you to everyone at Broadleaf Books for your patience and grace to extend my timeline out by a year. To my editor and friend Valerie—you have a heart of gold filled with compassion like no other. Thank you for your endless well of empathy and for showing up for me literally in Pennsylvania, which moved me to tears in front of five hundred people. I am lucky to know you.

To Carlos Whittaker and Rachel Cruze for making time to talk with me when you barely knew me. Thank you for sharing your wisdom.

To Gabbie Whitbeck for your heart and for vulnerably sharing your story so that others may know they are not alone.

To Tim Washer for making us laugh even while sharing your toughest moments and for always encouraging those around you.

To Lisa Fraidin, my "Hannukah humbug": thank you for always keeping it real—it's what I love most.

To Uncle Charlie Rivera for a lifetime of inspiration and allowing me to use your story.

To our village of therapists—Melanie Pearl, Charlie Manos, Nina Leventon, and Katie Greges: healing takes a village, and you were ours. Thank you for the support you gave to Ed, me, and our family during these years. This book would not have happened without all of you.

And to Kerin Tighe and the incredible educators, administrators, and nurses at Branchville Elementary who helped Carolina get back to herself: we are so grateful for each of you.

To Wanda Montes, Lisa Bollacke, and Carine Marco—the angels in our midst—for being there for us and literally praying us through these past few years. We saw miracles because of all of you.

To all of my friends and family who checked in on me, made me laugh, prayed and walked with me in real life or metaphorically: life is good because of you.

Finally, to Ed—for taking over when you needed to, waking me up off couches, charging my phone, and always believing in me. I am blessed to share this life with you. Natalia, Samuel, Sofia, and Carolina—even with our challenges, we hit the kid lottery with you four. You are our joy all year-round and continue to inspire us to be the parents you deserve.

I love you all so very much.

NOTES

Chapter 2: A Silent ~~Night~~ Morning

16 *mental health benefits of a morning ritual:* Morgan Smith, "3 Morning Habits to Help You Be Happier and More Productive at Work, According to Psychologists," *CNBC*, December 18, 2022, https://www.cnbc.com/2022/12/18/psychologists-morning-habits-to-help-you-be-happier-more-productive.html#:~:text=There%20are%20science%2Dbacked%20benefits,improve%20your%20productivity%20at%20work.

17 *Sunlight early in the day regulates our circadian rhythms:* Nathaniel M. Mead, "Benefits of Sunlight: A Bright Spot for Human Health," *Environmental Health Perspectives* 116, no. 5 (2008): 161–67, https://www.ncbi.nlm.nih.gov/pmc/articles/PMC2290997/.

19 *silence encourages the growth of cells in the hippocampus:* Timothy L. Gallati, "Where Silence Lives," *Harvard Divinity Bulletin*, Autumn/Winter 2017, https://bulletin.hds.harvard.edu/where-silence-lives/.

19 *constant noise increases our risk of high blood pressure, heart attacks, and even strokes:* L. Bernardi, C. Porta, and P. Sleight, "Cardiovascular, Cerebrovascular, and Respiratory Changes Induced by Different Types of Music in Musicians and Non-Musicians: The Importance of Silence," *Heart* 92, no. 4 (2006): 445–452.

Chapter 5: A Season of Thanksgiving

35 ***Brené Brown:*** "Brené Brown on Joy and Gratitude," *Global Leadership Network*, November 21, 2018, https://globalleadership.org/articles/leading-yourself/brene-brown-on-joy-and-gratitude/.

36 ***"gratitude actions" actually release different mood-elevating neurochemicals:*** Summer Allen, "The Science of Gratitude," *Greater Good Science Center*, May 1, 2018, https://search.issuelab.org/resource/the-science-of-gratitude.html.

36 ***Research shows that cardiac patients who kept gratitude journals for eight weeks had lower levels of inflammation***: Paul J. Mills and Laura Redwine, "Can Gratitude Be Good for Your Heart?" *Greater Good Magazine*, October 25, 2017, https://greatergood.berkeley.edu/article/item/can_gratitude_be_good_for_your_heart.

37 ***When cortisol is constantly high:*** Sean M. Smith and Wylie W. Vale, "The Role of the Hypothalamic-Pituitary-Adrenal Axis in Neuroendocrine Responses to Stress," *Dialogues in Clinical Neuroscience* 8, no. 4 (2006): 383–95, https://pmc.ncbi.nlm.nih.gov/articles/PMC3181830/.

Chapter 8: Angels in Our Midst

56 ***Christopher L. Kukk:*** *The Compassionate Achiever: How Helping Others Fuels Success* (HarperOne, 2017).

57 ***images of the brain during compassion:*** Barbora Kucerova et al., "From Oxytocin to Compassion: The Saliency of Distress," *Biology-Basel* 12, no. 2 (January

2023): 183, https://pmc.ncbi.nlm.nih.gov/articles/PMC9953150/.

Chapter 9: Choosing Joy

64 *The feelings of joy follow the actions of joy:* Barbara Bradley Hagerty, "Prayer May Reshape Your Brain . . . and Your Reality," *NPR: All Things Considered*, May 20, 2019, https://www.npr.org/2009/05/20/104310443/prayer-may-reshape-your-brain-and-your-reality.

64 *a five-minute meditation created by therapist Donald Altman:* Donald Altman, "Get G.L.A.D. and Scrub Away Rumination and Anxiety," *Psychology Today*, August 28, 2019, https://www.psychologytoday.com/us/blog/practical-mindfulness/201908/get-glad-and-scrub-away-rumination-and-anxiety.

Chapter 10: Finding Strength in Uncertainty

67 *response to people who offer well-intentioned but clueless cliches:* Anne Lamott, "It's Not So 'Terribly Strange to Be 70,'" *The Washington Post*, April 10, 2024, https://www.washingtonpost.com/opinions/2024/04/10/70th-birthday-check-in-aging/.

Chapter 12: Snapshot of the Sleigh Ride

77 *FOMO can result in very real physical and emotional symptoms:* Fatih Çelik and Behçet Yalin Özkara, "Fear

of Missing Out (FoMO) Scale: Adaptation to Social Media Context and Testing its Psychometric Properties," *Studies in Psychology* 42, no. 1 (2022): 71–103, https://avesis.ogu.edu.tr/yayin/efa08197-45b9-433a-913f-d6a19e894914/fear-of-missing-out-fomo-scale-adaptation-to-social-media-context-and-testing-its-psychometric-properties.

Chapter 15: Connected and Content

97 ***the Harvard Study of Adult Development:*** Liz Mineo, "Good Genes Are Nice, but Joy is Better," *Harvard Gazette*, April 11, 2017, https://news.harvard.edu/gazette/story/2017/04/over-nearly-80-years-harvard-study-has-been-showing-how-to-live-a-healthy-and-happy-life/.

97 ***Vivek Murthy declared a public health crisis of loneliness:*** U.S. Department of Health and Human Services, "New Surgeon General Advisory Raises Alarm about the Devastating Impact of the Epidemic of Loneliness and Isolation in the United States," May 3, 2023, https://www.hhs.gov/about/news/2023/05/03/new-surgeon-general-advisory-raises-alarm-about-devastating-impact-epidemic-loneliness-isolation-united-states.html.

Chapter 17: The Three Ds of Holiday Conflict

108 ***"God bless us, every one!":*** Charles Dickins, *A Christmas Carol* (London: Chapman & Hall, 1843), 58.

Chapter 18: Is Less Really More?

112 ***Forbes Advisor* reported in a 2023 survey:** Becky Pokora, "2023 American Holiday Spending Trends," *Forbes Advisor*, November 30, 2023, https://www.forbes.com/advisor/credit-cards/holiday-spending-trends-2023/#:~:text=Food%20and%20festive%20meals%20will,more%20in%20credit%20card%20debt.

Chapter 22: A Reset for the Season

134 ***Exercise such as jogging, doing jumping jacks, or taking a walk through a familiar neighborhood also allows for cognitive rest:*** "More Evidence that Exercise Can Boost Mood," *Harvard Health Publishing*, May 1, 2019, https://www.health.harvard.edu/mind-and-mood/more-evidence-that-exercise-can-boost-mood; Julia C. Basso and Wendy A. Suzuki, "The Effects of Acute Exercise on Mood, Cognition, Neurophysiology, and Neurochemical Pathways: A Review," *Brain Plasticity* 2, no. 2 (2017): 127–52, https://pmc.ncbi.nlm.nih.gov/articles/PMC5928534/.

135 ***The DMN is responsible for important functions:*** "Secret to Brain Success: Intelligent Cognitive Rest," *Harvard Health Publishing*, May 4, 2017, https://www.health.harvard.edu/blog/secret-to-brain-success-intelligent-cognitive-rest-2017050411705.

136 ***you cannot be anxious and sing at the same time:*** Stacy Horn, "Singing Changes Your Brain," *Time*, August 16, 2013, https://ideas.time.com/2013/08/16/singing-changes-your-brain/.

Chapter 24: Disappointing Gifts

145 ***Jeff Galak:*** "The Secret to Gift Giving," December 9, 2024, in *Hidden Brain*, podcast, 53:29, https://hiddenbrain.org/podcast/the-secret-to-gift-giving/.

Chapter 25: A Tale of Two Christmases

152 ***our brains synchronize with the people around us:*** Lydia Denworth, "Brain Waves Synchronize when People Interact," *Scientific American*, July 1, 2023, https://www.scientificamerican.com/article/brain-waves-synchronize-when-people-interact/; Chennan Lin et al., "Brains in Sync, Friends in Empathy: Interbrain Neural Mechanisms Underlying the Impact of Interpersonal Closeness on Mutual Empathy," *Proceedings of the Royal Society B 291*, no. 2031 (2024).

153 ***"name it to tame it" response:*** Magda Tabac, "Emotional Regulation: The (Simple) Neuroscience behind the 'Name It to Tame It' Technique," *Magda Tabac Mind Training*, updated January 31, 2024, https://magdatabac.com/name_it_to_tame_it/.

155 ***"Let them":*** Mel Robbins, *The Let Them Theory: A Life-Changing Tool That Millions of People Can't Stop Talking About* (Hay House, 2024).

Chapter 26: Presence over Presents

161 ***Limited attention spans translate into a limited ability to recall and remember:*** Caroline Leaf, "I'm a Neuroscientist and Here is Why You Need to Stop Multitasking,"

MindBodyGreen, October 9, 2020, https://www.mindbodygreen.com/articles/multitasking-brain-health.

162 **Anna Lembke:** *Dopamine Nation: Finding Balance in the Age of Indulgence* (Dutton, 2021).

Chapter 29: Wonder

177 **Carlos Whittaker:** *Reconnected: How 7 Screen Free Weeks with Monks and Amish Farmers Helped Me Recover the Lost Art of Being Human* (Nelson Books, 2024).

Chapter 31: New Year, Same Me

187 **only 9 percent of Americans who make New Year's resolutions actually keep them:** Richard Batts, "Why Most New Year's Resolutions Fail," *Ohio State University*, February 2, 2023, https://fisher.osu.edu/blogs/leadreadtoday/why-most-new-years-resolutions-fail.

188 **Melissa Kirsch:** "Resolving New Year's Resolutions," *New York Times*, January 6, 2024, https://www.nytimes.com/2024/01/06/briefing/resolving-new-years-resolutions.html.

188 **habit formation:** Benjamin Gardner, Phillippa Lally, and Jane Wardle, "Making Health Habitual: The Psychology of 'Habit-Formation' and General Practice," *British Journal of General Practice* 62, no. 605 (December 2012): 664–666, https://bjgp.org/content/62/605/664.

191 **James Clear:** *Atomic Habits: An Easy & Proven Way to Build Good Habits & Break Bad Ones* (Avery, 2018).